PLAYING BEYOND
THE NOTES

PLAYING BEYOND THE NOTES

A Pianist's Guide to Musical Interpretation

Deborah Rambo Sinn

OXFORD
UNIVERSITY PRESS

Oxford University Press is a department of the University of Oxford.
It furthers the University's objective of excellence in research, scholarship,
and education by publishing worldwide.

Oxford   New York
Auckland   Cape Town   Dar es Salaam   Hong Kong   Karachi
Kuala Lumpur   Madrid   Melbourne   Mexico City   Nairobi
New Delhi   Shanghai   Taipei   Toronto

With offices in
Argentina   Austria   Brazil   Chile   Czech Republic   France   Greece
Guatemala   Hungary   Italy   Japan   Poland   Portugal   Singapore
South Korea   Switzerland   Thailand   Turkey   Ukraine   Vietnam

Oxford is a registered trademark of Oxford University Press
in the UK and certain other countries.

Published in the United States of America by
Oxford University Press
198 Madison Avenue, New York, NY 10016

Library of Congress Cataloging-in-Publication Data
Sinn, Deborah Rambo.
Playing beyond the notes : a pianist's guide to musical interpretation / Deborah Rambo Sinn.
    p. cm.
Includes bibliographical references and index.
ISBN 978–0–19–985948–1 (hardcover : alk. paper) – ISBN 978–0–19–985950–4 (pbk. : alk. paper)
1. Piano music—Interpretation (Phrasing, dynamics, etc.)   2. Piano – Performance.
3. Piano—Instruction
and study.   I. Title.
MT220.S62 2013
786.2'146—dc23
2012035147

9 8 7 6 5 4 3 2 1
Printed in the United States of America
on acid-free paper

Contents

Contents

Musical Examples and Illustrations

Italics indicate a recorded example posted on the companion website.

Ex #	Composer	Title
1.1		Rubato Spectrum Illustration
1.2		Dynamic Spectrum Illustration
1.3	Beethoven	Sonata in F Major, op. 10, no. 2, I. Allegro
2.1	*Beethoven*	*Sonata in G Minor, op. 49, no. 2, I. Andante*
2.2	*J. S. Bach*	*Allemande from French Suite no. 6 in E Major, BWV 817*
2.3	*Beethoven*	*Sonata in A Major, op. 101, II. Lebhaft Marschmässig*
2.4	Haydn	Sonata in G Major, Hob. XVI: 27, I. Allegro con brio
2.5	Haydn	Sonata in G Major, Hob. XVI: 27, I. Allegro con brio
2.6	*Chopin*	*Nocturne in F♯ Major, op. 15, no. 2*
2.7	*Chopin*	*Nocturne in C♯ Minor, op. post.*
3.1	Chopin	Waltz in A Minor, op. 34, no. 2
3.2	*Chopin*	*Waltz in A Minor, op. 34, no. 2*
3.3	Chopin	Mazurka in G Minor, op. 24, no. 1
3.4	*Chopin*	*Mazurka in G Minor, op. 24, no. 1*
3.5	*Mozart*	*Sonata in C Major, K. 545, III. Rondo*
3.6	*Mozart*	*Sonata in F Major, K. 332, I. Allegro*
3.7	Chopin	Nocturne in B♭ Minor, op. 9, no. 1
3.8	*Chopin*	*Nocturne in B♭ Minor, op. 9, no. 1*

Ex #	Composer	Title
5.4	*Chopin*	*Nocturne in F Minor, op. 55, no. 1*
5.5	*Chopin*	*Nocturne in F Minor, op. 55, no. 1*
5.6	*Chopin*	*Nocturne in F Minor, op. 55, no. 1*
5.7	Chopin	Nocturne in F Minor, op. 55, no. 1
5.8	*Schubert*	*Sonata in A Major, D. 959, IV. Rondo*
5.9	Schubert	Sonata in A Major, D. 959, IV. Rondo
5.10	Beethoven	Sonata in B♭ Major, op. 22, IV. Rondo
5.11	*Beethoven*	*Sonata in B♭ Major, op. 22, IV. Rondo*
5.12	*Mozart*	*Sonata in C Major, K. 545, I. Allegro*
5.13	*Mozart*	*Sonata in C Major, K. 545, I. Allegro*
5.14	Mozart	Sonata in F Major, K. 332, II. Adagio
5.15	Mozart	Sonata in F Major, K. 332, II. Adagio
5.16	*Mozart*	*Sonata in F Major, K. 332, II. Adagio*
5.17	Mozart	Sonata in B♭ Major, K. 570, III. Rondo
5.18	Mozart	Sonata in B♭ Major, K. 570, III. Rondo
5.19	Beethoven	Sonata in G Major, op. 31, no. 1, I. Allegro vivace
5.20	Beethoven	Sonata in G Major, op. 31, no. 1, III. Rondo: Allegretto
5.21	*Beethoven*	*Sonata in F Minor, op. 2, no. 1, III. Prestissimo*
5.22	Beethoven	Sonata in F Major, op. 10, no. 2, I. Allegro
5.23	*Beethoven*	*Sonata in F Major, op. 10, no. 2, I. Allegro*
5.24	*Beethoven*	*Sonata in F Major, op. 10, no. 2, I. Allegro*
5.25	Mendelssohn	Venetianishes Gondelied in G Minor, op. 19, no. 6
5.26	*Mendelssohn*	*Venetianishes Gondelied in G Minor, op. 19, no. 6*
5.27	Beethoven	Sonata in G Major, op. 31, no. 1, III. Rondo: Allegretto
6.1	*R. Schumann*	*Hasche-Mann from Kinderscenen, op. 15*
6.2	R.Schumann	Hasche-Mann from Kinderscenen, op. 15
6.3	*Chopin*	*Nocturne in E Minor, op. 72, no. 1*
6.4	Chopin	Nocturne in E Minor, op. 72, no. 1
6.5	*Brahms*	*Intermezzo in A Major, op. 118, no. 2*
6.6	Brahms	Intermezzo in A Major, op. 118, no. 2
6.7	Brahms	Intermezzo in A Major, op. 118, no. 2
6.8	*Brahms*	*Intermezzo in A Major, op. 118, no. 2*
6.9	*Beethoven*	*Sonata in G Major, op. 79, II. Andante*
6.10	Beethoven	Sonata in B♭ Major, op. 22, I. Allegro con brio
6.11	*Chopin*	*Nocturne in G Minor, op. 37, no. 1*
6.12	Chopin	Nocturne in G Minor, op. 37, no. 1

Ex #	Composer	Title
7.1	*Mendelssohn*	*Lied ohne Worte, op. 62, no. 1*
7.2	Haydn	Sonata in C Major, Hob. XVI/50, I. Allegro
7.3	Haydn	Sonata in C Major, Hob. XVI/50, I. Allegro
7.4	Haydn	Sonata in C Major, Hob. XVI/50, I. Allegro
7.5	Mozart	Sonata in F Major, K. 332, III. Allegro assai
7.6	Mozart	Sonata in F Major, K. 332, III. Allegro assai
7.7	*Chopin*	*Mazurka in A Minor, op. 24, no. 2*
7.8	Chopin	Mazurka in A Minor, op. 24, no. 2
7.9	Chopin	Prelude in E Minor, op. 28, no. 4
7.10	*Chopin*	*Prelude in E Minor, op. 28, no. 4*
7.11	*J. S. Bach*	*Sarabande from French Suite no. 5 in G Major, BWV 816*
7.12	*Chopin*	*Mazurka in G Minor, op. 67, no. 2*
7.13	*Chopin*	*Nocturne in E Minor, op. post. 72, no. 1*
7.14	*Mozart*	*Sonata in F Major, K. 332, II. Adagio*
7.15	Mozart	Sonata in F Major, K. 332, II. Adagio
7.16		Trills Illustration
7.17		Turns Illustration
7.18		Turns and Trills Illustration
7.19	Mozart	Sonata in A Minor, K. 310, I. Allegro maestoso
7.20	J.S. Bach	Invention in D Minor, BWV 775
7.21	Beethoven	Sonata in C Major, op. 2, no. 3, I. Allegro con brio
7.22	Beethoven	Sonata in C Major, op. 2, no. 3, I. Allegro con brio
7.23	Beethoven	Sonata in C Major, op. 2, no. 3, I. Allegro con brio
7.24	*Beethoven*	*Sonata in C Major, op. 2, no. 3, I. Allegro con brio*
7.25	*Beethoven*	*Sonata in C Major, op. 2, no. 3, I. Allegro con brio*
7.26	*Beethoven*	*Sonata in C Major, op. 2, no. 3, I. Allegro con brio*
7.27	Mozart	Sonata in F Major, K. 332, II. Adagio
8.1	*Beethoven*	*Sonata in B♭ Major, op. 22, I. Allegro con brio*
8.2	Chopin	Nocturne in B♭ Minor, op. 9, no. 1
8.3	*Chopin*	*Nocturne in B♭ Minor, op. 9, no. 1*
8.4	Beethoven	Sonata in B♭ Major, op. 22, I. Allegro con brio
8.5	*Beethoven*	*Sonata in B♭ Major, op. 22, I. Allegro con brio*
8.6	*Beethoven*	*Sonata in C Minor, op. 13, II. Adagio cantabile*
8.7	Mozart	Sonata in F Major, K. 332, II. Adagio
8.8	*Mozart*	*Sonata in F Major, K. 332, II. Adagio*
8.9	*Mozart*	*Sonata in F Major, K. 332, I. Allegro*

Ex #	Composer	Title
8.10	*Schubert*	*Impromptu in G♭ Major, op. 90, no. 3*
8.11	*Beethoven*	*Sonata in G Major, op. 14, no. 2, I. Allegro*
8.12	*Chopin*	*Mazurka in B Minor, op. 33, no. 4*
8.13	*Chopin*	*Mazurka in B minor, op. 33, no. 4*
8.14	*Beethoven*	*Sonata in C Minor, op. 10, no. 1, III. Finale: Prestissimo*
8.15	*Haydn*	*Sonata in C Major, Hob. XVI:50, I. Allegro*
8.16	*Beethoven*	*Sonata in F Minor, op. 2, no. 1, IV. Prestissimo*
8.17	*Chopin*	*Nocturne in E♭ Major, op. 9, no. 2*
8.18	*Mozart*	*Sonata in C Minor, K. 467, I. Allegro*
8.19	*J. S. Bach*	*Prelude and Fugue in E♭ Major, W.T.C. I, BWV 852, Prelude*
8.20	Beethoven	Sonata in F Minor, op. 2, no. 1, I. Allegro
8.21	*Beethoven*	*Sonata in E♭ Major, op. 31, no. 3, II. Scherzo: Allegretto vivace*
8.22	*Haydn*	*Sonata in D Major, Hob. XVI: 37, I. Allegro con brio*
8.23	Chopin	Nocturne in B Major, op. 32, no. 1
8.24	Chopin	Nocturne in B Major, op. 32, no. 1
8.25	Chopin	Nocturne in C♯ Minor, op post.
8.26	*Chopin*	*Nocturne in C♯ Minor, op. post.*
8.27	Chopin	Waltz in A♭ Major, op. 69, no. 1
8.28	*Chopin*	*Waltz in A♭ Major, op. 69, no. 1*
8.29	Beethoven	Sonata in E♭ Major, op. 31, no. 3, I. Allegro
8.30	Chopin	Nocturne in F♯ Major, op. 15, no. 2
8.31	*Chopin*	*Nocturne in F♯ Major, op. 15, no. 2*
8.32	*Beethoven*	*Sonata in E♭ Major, op. 31, no. 3, I. Allegro*
8.33	Chopin	Nocturne in F♯ Major, op. 15, no. 2
8.34	*Chopin*	*Nocturne in F♯ Major, op. 15, no. 2*
9.1	*Mozart*	*Sonata in F Major, K. 332, I. Allegro*
9.2	*Mozart*	*Sonata in F Major, K. 332, I. Allegro*
9.3	Mozart	Sonata in F Major, I. Allegro
9.4	Mozart	Sonata in F Major, I. Allegro
9.5	*Schubert*	*Sonata in A Major, op. 120 (D. 664), I. Allegro moderato*
9.6	Schubert	Sonata in A Major, op. 120 (D. 664), I. Allegro moderato
9.7	Schubert	Sonata in A Major, op. 120 (D. 664), I. Allegro moderato
9.8	Schubert	Sonata in A Major, op. 120 (D. 664), I. Allegro moderato
9.9	Schubert	Sonata in A Major, op. 120 (D. 664), I. Allegro moderato
9.10	Schubert	Sonata in A Major, op. 120 (D. 664), I. Allegro moderato

Acknowledgements

None of this would have been possible without the solid training I received from my teachers, Menahem Pressler, James Tocco, and Leonard Mastrogiacomo. I was fortunate to study with each of you.

For this first time author full of questions and occasional frustrations, I could not have asked for a kinder and more supportive acquisitions editor than Todd Waldman at Oxford University Press. I am blessed that it was he who walked with me through this process.

My deep thanks go to Dr. Gary McRoberts, whose enthusiasm for, encouragement, and ongoing critiques of this project have steered me in all the right directions. Readers Tim Shafer, Adrienne Elisha, and Janna Johnson all gave me valuable input at just the right times.

My gratitude also goes to my students who have been gracious to me in this process. Special thanks go to Shannon, Julia, Annalise, Anna, Hunter, Darlene, and Ginny who will find their repertoire filling these pages.

Most importantly, I wish to thank my husband, Jerry, who has been my strongest supporter and head chef through it all.

About the Companion Website

www.oup.com/us/playingbeyondthenotes

To accompany *Playing Beyond the Notes,* we have created a website where readers can access more than 100 recordings performed by the author to bring life to the musical excerpts printed in this book. A combination of reading and listening will enhance the reader's experience. If a musical example is recorded, it will be signaled in the text with this symbol ◉. For the reader's reference, what follows is a full list of the musical examples and illustrations in the text—the examples in italics have been recorded and are available on the website.

Introduction

In our musical world, interpretive ideas and techniques are traditionally shared through demonstration by the teacher to the student, so it is a radical departure to propose that one can learn these concepts in a different way. This book departs from this convention as it makes musical interpretative ideas accessible in print. By systematizing the mechanics of interpretation, these chapters help the reader build a repertoire of basic skills that encompass centuries of compositional styles. Of course, when the muses visit a poet, words and phrases must be present and accessible. Similarly, for pianists, it is possible and desirable to have a large cache of interpretive options ready at the fingertips when the heart moves.

Performance practice and historical accuracy have often been the starting point for forcing boundaries around interpretation. Here, however, the approach is one of grasping the universal ideas around each element of music as it pertains to playing all piano music *first* before assigning good taste restrictions to particular works or composers. As an example, the process for producing a ritardando is the same for all pieces, irrespective of the composer. From there, it is just a matter of degree as to how broad or narrow the slowing-down process should be. This is true of most other subjects in music; it is the spectrum that changes, not the methodology.

This book is intended for performers, teachers, and advanced students who struggle with questions of interpretation. Those who find matters of expression an effortless task may also find the examples and checklists useful as they impart their skills to the next generation. The purpose is not to cover every potential interpretive dilemma but to provide enough examples to help musicians develop the basics, as well as the curiosity, to move beyond the last page and unearth deeper meanings behind the notes in the stack of scores waiting at the piano.

Each chapter focuses on a different element of musical interpretation, from how to end a piece successfully to the dynamic balances necessary to produce clarity in performance to the workings of usable rubato. The examples in this book are taken from intermediate to advanced piano literature and lean a bit toward music from the romantic era. This is intentional, as many pianists are more comfortable experimenting with Chopin than they are with Bach. Since true interpretive ideas are consistent throughout tonal music, one can take the expressive qualities learned for one composer and transfer those skills to another. The concepts in this book build from beginning to end, and the reader is encouraged to read it that way the first time through.

A number of different editions were consulted before the examples were generated. Although the notes are as true to the original as possible, some markings such as slurs, dynamics, and pedal indications were intentionally omitted. This streamlining cleans up the figures, forcing the focus onto the subject at hand. Although recordings of many of the examples can be found on the companion website, thorough comprehension will come from a combination of reading, listening, and experimentation at the piano.

Stepping into new territory is always a daunting task, and encouraging pianists to enthusiastically analyze scores seems even more challenging! The hope is that these pages will inspire performers and teachers alike to engage in a lifetime of exploration into the unlimited palette of sound.

ONE

The Score

NOTHING IS PERFECT

A discussion of musical interpretation should begin with the initial source from which pianists receive musical information: the score. The problem with scores, however, is that almost nothing in them is 100 percent reliable. Notes vary depending on editions, as do slurs, dynamic markings, and articulations. Adding to this uncertainty is that composers are limited by the constraints of squeezing an emotionally charged aural art form into a highly structured visual representation. This must be extremely frustrating and surely limits the amount of necessary information they are able to communicate. Layer onto this various performance practices, traditions, and popular interpretations. It is no wonder that teachers, students, and performers get caught up in the minutiae, miss the big picture, and forget that making great sound and communicating with one's audience should be the final goal.

How then does one sort through the notes and grab onto viable, moving, and breathing interpretations? Truthfully, interpretation does not change very much throughout tonal music. Performers lean on V^7 and relax on I. Every piece uses crescendos, agogic accents, articulations, and rubato. The range of what is acceptable hinges on a composer's era and intentions, but in a basic way *how* musicians use interpretive ideas in most pieces remains constant.

In Bach, for instance, the spectra (or ranges) for dynamics, tempos, and rubato are severely limited in scope compared to composers from the romantic era. The elements under consideration are the same though. Taking rubato as an example, the places in which rhythmic tension can be used are similar for Bach, Mozart, and Chopin, but the parameters of what is considered good taste (and consequently what works musically) change considerably with each composer. Figure 1.1 puts this concept into perspective.

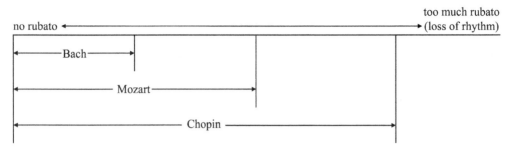

FIG. 1.1 *Rubato Spectrum Illustration*

Rubato should be used when playing the works of all three composers, just not in the same amounts. The bend in Bach is slight while that in Chopin can hover near the edge of rhythmic collapse. In practice, rubato could be similar for all three—*if* the extent to which each is performed is disregarded.

The dynamics spectrum for the same three composers might look like figure 1.2. Every aspect of music can be thought of in the same, fluid way. With this in mind and getting some distance from the exacting details of performance practice, the use of spectra is invaluable in creating a broad, overarching mindset in terms of interpretation.

Musical notation, which has sprung from centuries of traditions and acceptable practices, is remarkable but cannot tell the whole story. At the core, performers and teachers must work to find the truth behind every note of a piece by constantly questioning why a composer chose to write the way he or she did at that particular moment.

In the following seemingly straightforward example (fig. 1.3), a flood of questions come to mind. Why did Beethoven use this notation? Did he mean for the left-hand notes to last longer than those played by the right hand? Was it just easier to write it this way rather than some other way? Should the hands be even? How short should the notes in the left hand be? Why, in most editions, are staccatos written for the left hand when there are none in Beethoven's manuscript? Should it make a difference in interpretation that there are staccatos written in his manuscript for the parallel passage in the recapitulation, or was Beethoven just careless in his score preparation? Would it make a difference if he had written wedges instead of dots for staccato marks? Does it sound

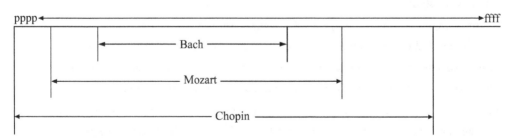

FIG. 1.2 *Dynamic Spectrum Illustration*

FIG. 1.3 *mm. 47–50, Sonata in F Major, op. 10, no. 2, I. Allegro, Beethoven*

better to play short staccatos as opposed to sticky ones? What type of piano did he own when this was written?

Of course, we may all arrive at different answers to most of these questions. Thank goodness! It allows us all to find a place in the musical world without sounding like cookie cutter pianists. If we can come to such varying conclusions, though, what guides us? Thorough scholarship and good taste are a great place to start, of course. Building a repertoire of convincing ways of playing any phrase, chord, or melody is crucial. As we build ideas and work out credible possibilities, we can pull these skills from the shelves and use them as needed.

One of my teachers once said that the worst thing a performer could do onstage was to be boring. It is crucial for questions to serve as constant sidekicks to our everyday practice regime. To simply let music happen without critical thought or curiosity is to be boring, and any pianist who does so is probably bored too. Score study is merely a means of determining what sounds best for a given piece, composer, and style. It is an exercise that strengthens a performer's ability to make, often spontaneously, convincing musical choices during performance. It is a living, exciting process that ultimately leads to strong connections between the performer and a composer's intentions. Every note of every piece should be approached with questions. Why this note here and now? How does it connect with those around it?

While confronting ambiguity in the score is just a part of a musician's challenge, it can lead to great discovery. At the heart of any piece ought to be a profound devotion to the way music sounds, and this should compel the performer to dig deeply.

TWO

Getting Started

To start playing a piece of music is a heavy responsibility. A tremendous amount of information must be communicated in the first few bars to successfully set up the tempo, meter, and character for the rest of the piece. Composers provide clues—in time signatures, tempo indications, dynamics, and metronome markings. Sadly, metronome markings are the single-most least-reliable element of any score, and, with rare exceptions, performers should disregard them. Other markings at the start of a piece should be considered as a whole and folded into an understanding of what a particular composer was trying to communicate. Since other insights can (and should) develop as one learns a piece, a flexible approach helps honor later inspiration that might not agree with first assessments.

CHARACTER

In this early Beethoven sonata (fig. 2.1), a quick look at the score elicits several questions as to how one might begin this piece. With a meter of 2/4, how does one keep the piece from sounding as if it is in 4/4 time? Part of the answer is discovering a tempo quick enough that it does not encourage the emphasis of each eighth note. Even though meter and tempo indications often fall to hard definitions, in reality they are about character rather than strict guidelines. Meter and tempo work together to create and define the personality and atmosphere of a piece. In this sonata, it would be easy to let the mood sink into plodding despair if the two elements are not taken into account as a team.

EXTRAMUSICAL INFLUENCES

More obvious examples of this cooperative effort between tempo and time signature are found when the composer points to a particular dance form and its temperament. Bach,

Andante

🔊 **FIG. 2.1** *mm. 1–8, Sonata in G Minor, op. 49, no. 2, I. Andante, Beethoven*

for example, did not use tempo markings as a rule, but in his suites, each type of dance has idiosyncrasies that should affect choices in tempo and character. Every dance is tied to an identifying meter, such as the allemande (a favorite opening piece for his suites) with its quadruple time signature and moderate tempo (fig. 2.2). A performer should communicate the meter and character, along with a clear presentation of the allemande's typical two-voice imitative structure, in such a way that a knowledgeable listener could identify the type of dance by hearing just a few bars. A list of common dance forms, including the allemande, can be found in the glossary.

Other instances occur when composers extend a tempo marking to include an extramusical or programmatic description such as in this Beethoven sonata (fig. 2.3). The combination of *Marschmässig* or *alla Marcia* to a quadruple meter should lead a performer to a different attitude toward this movement's dotted rhythms and rests than would a tempo marking of simply *Lebhaft* or *vivace*. Beethoven's indication

🔊 **FIG. 2.2** *mm. 1–4, Allemande from French Suite no. 6 in E Major, BWV 817, J. S. Bach*

Lebhaft Marschmässig
Vivace alla Marcia

FIG. 2.3 *mm. 1–4, Sonata in A Major, op. 101, II. Lebhaft Marschmässig, Beethoven*

to play this work in a lively manner while keeping it in the character of a march presents a challenging task but also narrows the field of tempos that would work to accomplish both.

SETTING THE METER

Pieces that begin with an upbeat or upbeats are problematic and often played inaccurately. The note is either too long or too short, or accented in such a way that the upbeat sounds like a downbeat. This is especially true when the upbeat's note value is different from that of the following note(s) in this Haydn sonata (fig. 2.4). Communicating the meter and tempo clearly is impossible if the first note is not rhythmically exact. Additionally, the upbeat must not be accented in any way but should be used to give energy and attention to the downbeat that follows (fig. 2.5). The meter is always easier to establish in the ears of the audience when the first beats of the first few measures of a piece are solid and unbending.

This Chopin nocturne (fig. 2.6) demonstrates another concern. As the piece progresses, rhythm becomes increasingly more complex and, with it, the slippery rubato

Allegro con brio

FIG. 2.4 *mm. 1–5a, Sonata in G Major, Hob. XVI: 27, I. Allegro con brio, Haydn*

FIG. 2.5 *mm. 1–2, Sonata in G Major, Hob. XVI: 27, I. Allegro con brio, Haydn*

that is sure to accompany it. With few exceptions, playing with strict tempo and rhythm, devoid of rubato, works well at the beginning of a piece until the meter and tempo are clearly communicated. This approach provides a solid foundation and sets a standard for tempo and character. Once these elements are established, the performer can begin using

FIG. 2.6 *mm. 1–12, Nocturne in F♯ Major, op. 15, no. 2, Chopin*

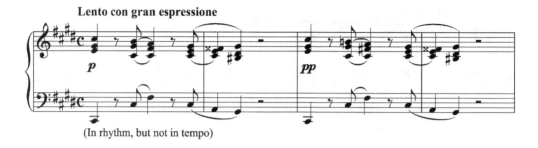

(In rhythm, but not in tempo)

(Set tempo here)

FIG. 2.7 *mm. 1–8, Nocturne in C♯ Minor, op. post., Chopin*

a rubato consistent with performance practices appropriate to the work and composer. The nocturne's second presentation of the theme, just nine measures into the piece, is a wild ride rhythmically. With the tempo of the first measures still in the ears of the audience, these later measures can be flung wide in their interpretation without losing the structure of the piece. Unless a piece begins in an unstable way, such as with a cadenza or fantasia-type opening, one should consider playing the first few measures in a way that outlines meter and tempo in a clear and direct manner.

By contrast, the nocturne in figure 2.7 starts with an uneasy introduction that does not have anything to do with the rest of the piece besides establishing the key. In cases such as this or when the opening is written in a fantasia style, tempo can be set later with the arrival of the main theme. Although it is possible to play this four-bar introduction in tempo, it is not particularly compelling. Waiting to set the tempo until the main theme begins allows the performer to express the tentativeness of this peculiar introduction.

Although these examples provide a good starting point, a successful interpretation is ultimately governed by a multitude of elements, including what happens in the rest of the work. A tempo that seems perfect at first may not work for the entire piece and must be adjusted to accommodate phrasing or clarity in a later section. Eventually, a performer must discover the equilibrium that leads to a convincing tempo for the complete work.

CHECKLIST FOR CHAPTER 2

- What is the edition being used?
  - Is it heavily edited?
  - Are other editions available for comparison?
- What tempo best reflects the character of the piece?
  - How does the tempo marking point to character traits in the piece?
  - Does the tempo work for the whole piece?
- What questions need to be addressed before starting a piece?
  - Is there a dance form associated with the piece?
  - If so, what is it? How does this affect the way the piece should be played?
  - Are there extramusical (programmatic) elements or indications?
- Does the piece begin with an upbeat?
  - If so, is it being played in time?
- Does the piece start with a cadenza or with a fantasia-type opening (free)?
  - If not, has the tempo been carefully set for the piece in the first few measures?
  - If so, at what point should a tempo be set?

THREE

The End

RITARDANDO

"Just slow down!" is the only instruction many receive from their earliest piano teachers on how to end a piece. There are a number of factors that make ending a piece more complex and ultimately more interesting than that, but conversely, it is one of the easiest concepts to grasp.

For example, exactly when should this Chopin waltz begin to slow down (fig. 3.1)? Additionally, how does a performer indicate that it is actually the end of the piece as this exact cadence shows up twice previously?

Before deciding, one should reconsider the folklore surrounding ending a piece of music. One concept taught is that the relationship between notes should remain constant through a ritardando. For example, a quarter note should always have a quarter note value, easily and precisely divided into two eighths, and a ritardando has to maintain these relationships while slowing down. One can bend but never break rhythm is the advice, a principle that many ritardandos can follow. However, there are times when breaking rhythm is exactly what is required to create clarity. Delaying the final beat of the waltz, for instance, gives the listener the unambiguous, visceral sign that there will be no more music after that point. The slight delay needed to set the last chord apart brings to the audience an expectation that something important is about to happen. This, in turn, allows them to experience the ending of the piece *with* the performer and not as an afterthought. It is far better for listeners to feel anticipation for "What's about to happen?" rather than confused by "What just happened?"

This example presents another challenge because of the slow tempo. If the ritardando is begun too soon, one risks "putting the baby to sleep too early" (a favorite saying of one of my teachers). Because of the slow pace in this particular piece, a listener will more

(Lento)

FIG. 3.1 *last four measures, Waltz in A Minor, op. 34, no. 2, Chopin*

slight delay/out of tempo
without a break in the sound

pp

ritardando begins here

FIG. 3.2 *last four measures, Waltz in A Minor, op. 34, no. 2, Chopin*

quickly detect a change in the tempo if it comes from faster-moving notes, in this case eighths, than slower ones. The optimal place to begin slowing down in this piece, then, is five beats from the last chord (fig. 3.2). The ritardando should be gradual, with the last chord set out of place with a slight delay and without any break in the legato line.

STRUCTURAL ENDINGS

The following mazurka (fig. 3.3) poses a more challenging question. Where does the piece really end? Even though this might seems like a rhetorical question, it is not. The strength of the V^7 chord resolving to I (with both chords in root position) straddling the last barline suggests that the first beat and not the second is the structural, or "real," ending of the piece (fig. 3.4). Therefore, the first beat is set and the second beat played and heard as an afterthought. If the first and lowest note of the rolled chord, G, is played simultaneously with the right-hand note, the cadence is further strengthened with the root of the chord occurring on the downbeat. As an added benefit, playing the rolled chord in this way avoids pedaling issues. Playing the first two notes before the beat ensures that the pedal will not catch the bottom note, weakening the cadence and sounding like a musical hiccup. The ritenuto (ritardando), beginning three measures from the end, gradually slows the piece through the first beat of the last measure, which should be played slightly out of time (fig. 3.4).

(Lento)

FIG. 3.3 *last four measures, Mazurka in G Minor, op. 24, no. 1, Chopin*

FIG. 3.4 *last four measures, Mazurka in G Minor, op. 24, no. 1, Chopin*

Although the preceding example has only one extra beat, other pieces have longer "post-ending" endings. How does one determine where the structural ending is exactly? Who can forget the pages of back-and-forth oscillation between I and V^7 chords in the last movement of Beethoven's Fifth Symphony? The structural ending in that piece comes quite early—at the coda with eighty-three measures to go. Although composers write all types of endings, there are a few reliable indicators for finding this junction. If there is a coda, then the structural ending almost always occurs at the beginning of that section. Otherwise, a strong V-I cadence or, better, a I^6_4-V-I near the end of the piece could signal another possibility.

Figures 3.5 and 3.6 are examples from the endings of two Mozart sonata movements. In the first, the structural ending occurs at the end of the rondo theme using a cadence heard earlier in the piece. The difference in this instance is its juxtaposition with the coda. Likewise, in the second example (in sonata form without a coda), the same cadence also appears earlier, albeit in a different key. The structural ending here is where the second theme meets the closing theme. In each, many measures of music remain before the pieces end.

Finding the structural ending allows a performer to put the complete conclusion of a work into context for an audience. Sometimes the event with the greatest emphasis in a work is at the structural ending, so determining the outlines of a work's ending is paramount to its successful interpretation.

THE TECHNIQUE OF SLOW-FAST-SLOW

The action stops with an atypical structural ending with a weak $vii°^7$-I cadence in this Chopin nocturne (fig. 3.7). He used a Picardy third for the last few chords, ending the

FIG. 3.5 *last seventeen measures, Sonata in C Major, K. 545, III. Rondo, Mozart*

work in B♭ major (I) rather than B♭ minor (i), the key of the piece (fig. 3.7). After the dramatic, falling diminished chord of the previous measure, the B♭ major chord is unexpected and startling, turning an ordinarily weak cadence into a strong one with its jolting harmonies.

The repeated B♭ major chords could easily bore both the performer and listener. Chopin added some variety with the interloping G♭ on the penultimate beat, but otherwise the listener (without score in hand) does not know which chord might be the final one. Even though a performer is past the structural ending of a piece, being clear until the very end is still important. The last, rolled chord played in a rhythmically even way can be terribly dull. Playing it this way also gives no indication that it is the last event, and a listener might expect even more chords to follow it. Playing the rolled chord in a slow-fast-slow way can signal the end and add interest and movement to the chord. The notes that are brought forward as a result are the lowest and highest ones; in this case, these are the root (B♭) and the third (D♮) of the chord.

FIG. 3.6 *last ten measures, Sonata in F Major, K. 332, I. Allegro, Mozart*

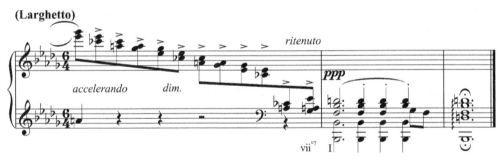

FIG. 3.7 *last three measures, Nocturne in B♭ Minor, op. 9, no. 1, Chopin*

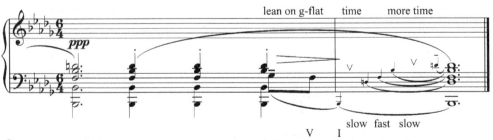

FIG. 3.8 *last two measures, Nocturne in B♭ Minor, op. 9, no. 1, Chopin*

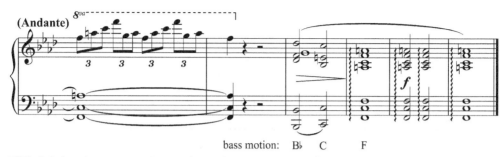

FIG. 3.9 *last six measures, Nocturne in F Minor, op. 55, no. 1, Chopin*

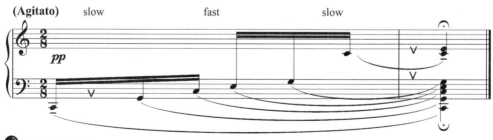

FIG. 3.10 *last three measures, Nocturne in F Minor, op. 55, no. 1, Chopin, rolled chords*

The bass motion IV-V-I (B♭-C-F) points to the structural ending in a different Chopin nocturne (figure 3.9). The fast-slow-fast principle can apply to the performance of the last three measures as a whole. The symbol for the rolled chords varies from edition to edition in this spot: some run the length of the whole chord, as in figure 3.9, and others separate into two sections with their markings disconnected between the clefs. So, should one play the chord from top to bottom or roll the hands simultaneously? It depends on the desired sound, so experimenting with the options is a good way to determine which is better in a given situation. In this example, playing the chords hand to hand gives the performer a wonderful palette for expression that would be severely limited by rolling the hands together. Figure 3.10 demonstrates how this also lends a melodic treatment to these rolled chords and allows for a beautifully expressive ending.

The end of this Chopin prelude can be treated in a similar fashion, although its broken chord is written out in sixteenth notes rather than by a broken chord symbol (fig. 3.11).

FIG. 3.11 *last two measures, Prelude in C Major, op. 28, no.1, Chopin*

FIG. 3.12 *last four measures, Prelude in A♭ Major, op. 28, no. 17, Chopin*

Emphasis should fall on the first and last notes, affording the chord a full sound that keeps pushing energy through from the second note of the chord to the last.

A different type of slow-fast-slow technique is useful at the end of the Chopin Prelude in A♭ Major (fig. 3.12). A V-I cadence, several measures from the end of the piece, points to the structural ending. This is followed by a series of repeated A♭ major chords. To keep these from bogging down, a slow-fast-slow treatment works to keep the notes energized.

WHEN WILL IT END?

Occasionally, a piece creates chaos with an ending that does not easily or naturally come to a stop. For most of the Raindrop Prelude, the listener is bombarded with repeated A♭s or G♯s in the same register—just below middle C (fig. 3.13). The note is repeated more than 450 times throughout the piece. In a few instances other musical ideas attempt to enter, but the repeated notes always return. Starting eleven measures from the end, Chopin wrote *smorzando* and *slentando*, followed by an odd two-measure cadenza, an early down-shift of the tempo with so many measures left. Although there is no *a tempo* indicated after this, it is intuitive to resume the original tempo in the measure after the cadenza. With six measures and numerous A♭s to go before the double barline, not increasing the tempo threatens forward momentum. Chopin marks a ritenuto two measures from the end. Although these five beats might not seem long enough, slowing down any sooner would prove an early death to the piece.

When arriving at the end of the piece, how does one communicate, "This time, I'm serious! No more A♭s," especially since they drive right up and into the last measure? Chopin provides help by stalling further harmonic development with two V-I bass note cadences in the last three measures. In the first, the rising figure creates the weaker of the two cadences. In the second one, the bass notes fall, and it is this stronger motion that points to the structural ending (fig. 3.14). An effective interpretation would include a significant ritardando in the penultimate measure with a delay before playing the final chord.

FIG. 3.13 *last fourteen measures, Prelude in D♭ Major, op. 28, no. 15, Chopin*

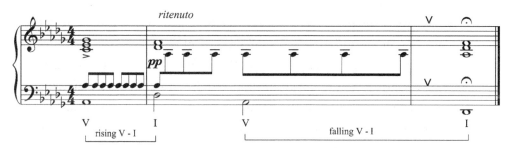

FIG. 3.14 *last three measures, Prelude in D♭ Major, op. 28, no. 15, Chopin*

THE PROBLEM WITH RESTS

Rests occurring toward the end of a piece or at any point in the music where the tempo is changing, if not worked out carefully, can pose difficulties when communicating rhythmic clarity to one's audience. How should ritardandos be treated when long rests occur? What

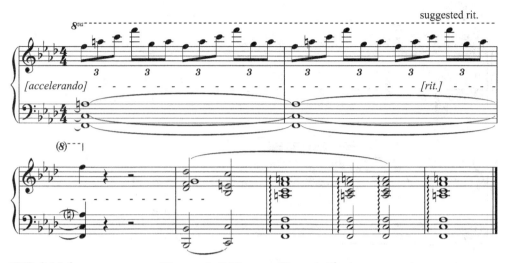

FIG. 3.15 *last seven measures, Nocturne in F Minor, op. 55, no. 1, Chopin*

does one do when faced with the absence of rhythmic impulse? A long rest, five measures from the end of this nocturne, brings these challenges to the performer (fig. 3.15). In this case, a nine-measure cadenza-like passage precedes the rest. While there are seven sets of a repeated pattern with an accelerando written through to the end of them, common sense (even without instruction from the composer) dictates a slight ritardando to wind these down. That determined, the last triplets of the repeated pattern set the rate at which a performer slows down through to the next measure. The ritardando must continue through the rests and include the first beat of the next measure. It is possible to continue slowing down after this point, but it is not advisable to change the tempo in the middle of a period of rest. To do so would destroy the rhythmic relationships already in the ears of the audience.

Sometimes a composer offers a challenge to a performer's natural instincts as Schubert does in this sonata, where a full measure of rest follows the structural ending (fig. 3.16). Making an unusual composition choice, he did not use a fermata but rather exact values for this rest. If one makes a ritardando at the cadence and continues it through the rest, the tempo becomes unbearably slow just at the moment when the piece takes on longer rhythmic values. Doing so also forces the last six measures into an unbearable slumbering tempo. This might be tolerable if the piece ended quickly thereafter, but Schubert heads directly for a deceptive cadence that extends the piece an additional three bars. The best solution, surprisingly, is to make no ritardando before the rest at the structural ending. As is the case here, it is important to analyze a large section to determine an overall strategy for ending a work. First instincts may not lead to a practical interpretation.

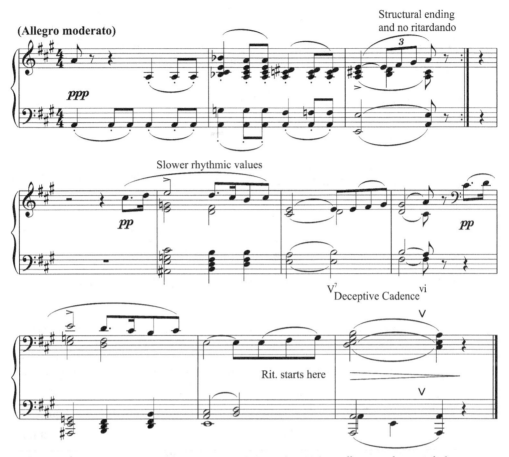

FIG. 3.16 *last ten measures, Sonata in A Major, op. 120 (D. 664), I. Allegro moderato, Schubert*

MIXING IT UP RHYTHMICALLY

Pieces that end with mixed rhythms need special attention, such as in the two measures of this Chopin mazurka (fig. 3.17). Since duplets are mixed in with triplets, finding an appropriate place to start a ritardando is vital. If a ritardando begins at triplets preceded by duplets, the result might lead the listener to believe that duplets were still in play as

FIG. 3.17 *last four measures, Mazurka in E Minor, op. 17, no. 2, Chopin*

FIG. 3.18 *last four measures, Mazurka in E Minor, op. 17, no. 2, Chopin, wrong rhythm*

demonstrated in figure 3.18. This destroys the accuracy of the rhythmic shift (duplets to triplets) causing a listener to lose the barline in the ensuing chaos and is followed by confusion at the end of the piece when nothing lines up as expected. Several editions mark the ritardando beginning three measures from the end on beat two, but given the slow tempo, this is too early. It would be better to start the ritardando as shown in figure 3.19 to maintain the integrity of the triplets and to slow the piece in a clear way. The last note should arrive slightly late as in other examples in this chapter.

NO RITARDANDO NECESSARY

There are a few times when no ritardando at all is the best choice. Here are two examples from early Beethoven sonatas where none would be required because of their whirlwind endings. In the first (fig. 3.20), he slowed the rhythmic impulse down with whole notes toward the end. He followed this with quarter note chords in aggravated off-beat accents

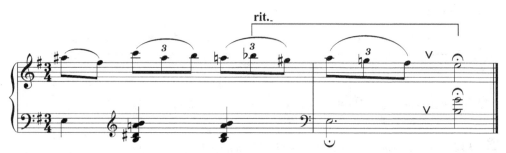

FIG. 3.19 *last two measures, Mazurka in E Minor, op. 17, no. 2, Chopin*

FIG. 3.20 *last eight measures, Sonata in F Minor, op. 2, no. 1, I. Allegro, Beethoven*

starting four measures from the end that finally find their footing in the last three chords. Because the skewed accents toss the meter into chaos in earlier measures, playing these three chords in strict time restores the rhythm to its proper metrical place. Adding a ritardando would destroy the excitement of this ending and should be avoided.

Beethoven composed starts and stops in the last twenty measures of this rondo (fig. 3.21), a style of writing often found in transitional material in his later works. As the piece heads for the end, ostensibly to C major, a long D/E trill abruptly ends on a D♯, which has nothing to do with the trill or with the key of C (except to thwart it). Phrases in A major and A minor show up before the key lands on its feet again at the *a tempo*. The fermatas occurring on rests, reminiscent of Haydn's grand pauses, are regrouping points, as if to say, "This isn't working. How else can this piece get back on track?" At the end of the A minor run, a V-I cadence in C major can be found, but the chords are in weak inversions. Finally, in the last line, C major is solidly established. Although a V⁷-I chord relationship appears with the octave scale passage (starting seven measures from the end), a much stronger V⁷-I cadence is at the end of the piece, at its structural ending. A built-in ritardando is created with the sudden reduction of rhythmic impulse to one chord per measure in the last three bars. This slowing rhythm, combined with the exuberance of finding C major after such a harmonic struggle, would indicate that no ritardando is necessary or even desirable.

The rhythmic impulse does not change in this next example, but Beethoven uses a disappearing ending in this sonata with a G major arpeggio (fig. 3.22). There is no written ritardando, and none is needed.

La fille aux cheveux lin (The Girl with the Flaxen Hair), Debussy indicates *perdendo* for one measure only. The remaining four measures dissolve with just a few notes here and there, so no additional manipulation of tempo is necessary.

FIG. 3.21 *last 20 measures, Sonata in C Major, op. 2, no. 3, IV. Allegro assai, Beethoven*

The skills learned for ending a piece successfully can be used as a basis for tackling other interpretive challenges. As examples, knowing how to use a ritardando effectively is vital for building rubato, and understanding rhythmic pulses and connections helps to develop bass lines. Musical elements, disparate in nature but nevertheless connected,

(Presto alla tedesca)

FIG. 3.22 *last seven measures, Sonata in G Major, op. 79, I. Presto alla tedesca, Beethoven*

are like a mobile—each has an influence over, and affects how another is performed. Understanding how everything moves and breathes together ultimately helps maintain the balance of a piece.

(Très calme et doucement expressif)

FIG. 3.23 *last four measures, La fille aux cheveux lin, Debussy*

CHECKLIST FOR CHAPTER 3

- Has the composer indicated a ritardando?
  - If not, is there a need for one?
  - If not and if it would be appropriate to include one, where should it start?
  - If so, do other editions include it and does it appear in the same place?
  - Should one move an existing ritardando to a different beat or measure in order to maintain rhythmic clarity?
- Is there a structural ending?
  - What should one look for as signs of a structural ending in a piece?
- Are there stagnant passages or rolled chords that could use a slow-fast-slow treatment?
- Does the piece threaten to end several times before it actually does?
  - If so, what techniques can be employed to ensure clarity and keep the piece from getting bogged down too early?
- Are there rhythmic elements that affect where the ritardando should start?
  - Are there slowing rhythmic values that would destroy the momentum of the piece if a ritardando is started too early?
  - Are there rests or mixed rhythms (such as duplets plus triplets) that need special attention?
- Would using a ritardando negatively change the character of the music in its final measures?
  - Is the line disappearing at the end due to the slowing of rhythmic impulse, either by notes or rests?

FOUR

Boxes and Beams

BOXES

There is a delicate balance between meter with its hierarchical natural accents and the push of melodic phrases and rhythmic gestures beyond the barline. Slur marks are often suspect and may or may not lead to suitable phrase choices (chapter 9 will address this issue in greater detail). Other visual cues are equally unwieldy. Unfortunately, what musicians see on the page does not immediately translate into how a piece should be played, so an understanding of how composers fight against the constraints of the written score is one of the most important aspects of score study.

Musical notes are strung together with beams and separated into boxes. Visually this is a helpful organizational device for such elements as meter and rhythm, but for musicians the challenge is playing in a way that does not sound boxy. Teachers already know how students get to the end of a measure or line and come to a full stop before moving forward, insuring a sputtering musical disaster. Composers have struggled for years to push past the barline and to communicate these wishes to musicians, but sometimes the music writing conventions of the times thwart their best efforts.

Not that Bach was the first or last to fight the barline, but his music is a good place to start. In this prelude from his Well-Tempered Clavier (fig. 4.1), the melodic phrases begin on the second sixteenth note and end on either beat three or beat one in both hands. Because of the long notes that separate them, these groupings are recognizable at first glance.

In the gigue from the French Suite in G Major, these groupings can be difficult to see because of the motoristic, unrelenting rhythm. Unlike the previous prelude, Bach used an upbeat to start this work, providing the first crucial piece of information toward understanding its subphrases (fig. 4.2). From this point on, each grouping of notes starts with

FIG. 4.1 *mm. 1–3, Prelude from Prelude and Fugue in E♭ Major, W.T.C. I, BWV 852, J. S. Bach*

an upbeat. He continued developing similar phrase patterns throughout the entire piece, typical of his compositional style known as Fortspinnung.

The brackets in figure 4.3 show how the piece was crafted and which notes belong together musically. Does this mean the performer must cultivate a style that points out each of these subphrases? Of course not, but understanding how the piece is structured should and will influence how it is ultimately interpreted through the use of dynamics and longer phrase choices.

To overcome the difficulties that barlines present, composers over many generations chose to begin countless phrases in one of the two ways demonstrated in the previous examples—just after the start of a measure or with an upbeat. Each pushes the phrase past its barlines, avoiding patterns starting on the downbeat and/or ending with the last note of the measure. An interesting balance is struck in acknowledging these inner connections while maintaining the hierarchy of the meter with natural accents that fall on strong beats. It is the single most important skill a pianist needs: the ability to guide music forward while never allowing the meter to unintentionally disappear.

Mozart started this sonata movement with a Hammerstroke in the left hand to establish both the key and the downbeat (fig. 4.4), but the melodic gesture begins on the offbeat with forward momentum generated by a series of rhythmically identical groupings (fig. 4.5). Even with a fast tempo, identifying the subphrases gives energy and interest to the melodic line in a way that pushes past the beats and barlines.

FIG. 4.2 *mm. 1–3, Gigue from French Suite in G Major, BWV 816, J. S. Bach*

FIG. 4.3 *mm. 1–3, Gigue from French Suite in G Major, BWV 816, J. S. Bach, phrase marks added*

FIG. 4.4 *mm. 1–3a, Sonata in F Major, K. 332, III. Allegro assai, Mozart*

FIG. 4.5 *mm. 1–3a, Sonata in F Major, K. 332, III. Allegro assai, Mozart, subphrase markings added*

SHORT TO LONG

Mozart also began the first movement of the same sonata on the downbeat (fig. 4.6), but he skillfully employed another compositional technique to propel this phrase forward in a way different from the previous examples. Unless otherwise noted by a composer, short notes give energy to the longer notes that follow. Here, the quarter note in the third beat of each of the first three measures pushes the phrase past the barline and into the next measure to a half note, a strategy repeated throughout the piece (fig. 4.7). In a simple manner, Mozart balanced phrasing and meter here with beautiful elegance. The left hand maintains the integrity of the downbeats while the right hand pushes the phrase from measure to measure.

FIG. 4.6 *mm. 1–5a, Sonata in F Major, K. 332, I. Allegro, Mozart*

FIG. 4.7 *mm. 1–5a, Sonata in F Major, K. 332, I. Allegro, Mozart*

BEAMS

The way music is beamed and otherwise visually grouped can give false clues just as easily as measures and barlines do. Yet dotted eighth notes are beamed with sixteenth notes—two notes that almost never have a connected rhythmic impulse. Each sixteenth really "belongs" to the following dotted eighth (fig. 4.8).

In figure 4.9, the momentum of Beethoven's funeral march relies on the sixteenth moving toward and giving energy to the next dotted eighth note. These musical connections might be easier to understand without using beams and barlines (fig. 4.10). Visually, this makes no sense at all, of course. It is impossible to keep track of beats and meter looking at this example. Thankfully, written music is formatted with visual clarity in mind, but performers must continually reorganize what is seen into what should be heard.

The musical regrouping of notes is usually necessary with dotted rhythms but also extends to a wide variety of other rhythmic circumstances as illustrated in the 6/8 example from Mendelssohn (fig. 4.11). Understanding this concept transforms the piece when eighth notes push out of their beats and measures, giving energy to the quarter notes that follow. Usually in 6/8 time, beat three acts as an upbeat to four and beat six as an upbeat to one (fig. 4.12).

FIG. 4.8 *Dotted Eighths and Sixteenth Notes*

MARCIA FUNEBRE sulla morte d'un Eroe
Maestoso andante

FIG. 4.9 *mm. 1–2, Sonata in A♭ Major, op. 26, III. Marcia Funebre, Beethoven*

FIG. 4.10 *mm. 1–2, Sonata in A♭ Major, op. 26, III. Marcia Funebre, Beethoven, beams and barlines removed*

(Andante sostenuto)

🔊 **FIG. 4.11** *mm. 7b–11a, Venetianishes Gondelied in G Minor, op. 19, no. 6, Mendelssohn*

FIG. 4.12 *mm. 7b–11a, Venetianishes Gondelied in G Minor, op. 19, no. 6, Mendelssohn*

Although note values and tempo are different in the Rondo Capriccioso (fig. 4.13), the same principles of 6/8 apply. The hands trade off playing the theme and accompaniment. In each, there are strong motions from beat three to four and from beat six to one.

In a more complex example, Chopin used a variety of short-to-long combinations to keep forward momentum in this mazurka (fig. 4.14). After setting the tempo and meter in the first few beats, he bridged over the barlines using eighth notes as upbeats as in previous examples. Additionally, he used a sixteenth note rhythm to drive energy into beat

(Presto leggiero)

🔊 **FIG. 4.13** *mm. 27–30, Rondo Capriccioso, op. 14, Mendelssohn*

FIG. 4.14 *mm. 1–4, Mazurka in C Major, op. 33, no. 3, Chopin*

FIG. 4.15 *mm. 11b–13a, Prelude in E Minor, op. 28, no. 4, Chopin*

two, a naturally accented beat in many mazurkas. These small connections occur on all levels of the music, melodically and harmonically; the examples here only begin to hint at these first-level rhythmic sets.

THE FOUR NOTES OF A TRIPLET

Another rhythm that creates difficulties because of groupings and beams is the triplet. Visually, a separation exists between the triplet and the following note, but in performance, these four notes connect both musically and rhythmically. In figures 4.15 and 4.16 from the Prelude in E Minor by Chopin, brackets span the full four-note gesture of the triplet.

Although attaching the triplet with the fourth note is imperative, connecting the triplet with what precedes it might be an important consideration as well. In this nocturne (fig. 4.17), the triplet connects each time with an upbeat—the first time with an eighth

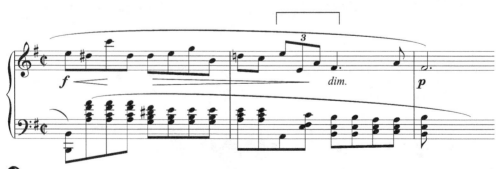

FIG. 4.16 *mm. 17–19a, Prelude in E Minor, op. 28, no. 4, Chopin*

FIG. 4.17 *mm. 1–5a, Nocturne in G Minor, op. 37, no. 1, Chopin*

note and the second time with a sixteenth. These notes should be included in the entire gesture, which includes five notes.

Similarly, the quintuplet in figure 4.18 links to the notes on both sides.

The examples here represent only a few rhythmic connections that composers use to keep music moving forward and to demonstrate how the visual art of music writing can deceive. Learning how composers used rhythm links is the starting point of developing good phrases. A more in-depth discussion of how composers maintain musical balance on this interesting tightrope of meter and phrasing continues with more intricate examples in chapter 9.

FIG. 4.18 *mm. 19–20a, Nocturne in B Major, op. 32, no. 1, Chopin*

CHECKLIST FOR CHAPTER 4

- How do phrases really divide, regardless of slurs?
  - Are there repeating rhythmic patterns? If so, how do they divide?
  - Do they begin on an upbeat?
  - Do they begin after beat one (the second sixteenth note, for example)?
- Are there obvious short-to-long relationships, such as eighth notes to quarter notes?
  - How are these used to move the music forward and past barlines?
  - Are there other short-to-long relationships, such as dotted rhythms?
  - What is the best way to play them so they sound connected from short to long?
- Is the piece in 6/8 time?
  - If so, what is the best way to connect beats three to four and beats six to one?
- Are there triplets or other beamed or note groupings where the whole musical gesture includes notes that appear before and/or after them?
- Does the music move in a natural way over the beams and barlines when played?

FIVE

Voicing from the Bottom Up

Often the only attention in teaching given to voicing is to bring out the melody, most often found at the top of the right hand. While this is a crucial element of playing, there is another "melody" in the bass that needs to be nurtured to develop good overall balance in playing. If just the right hand is voiced, the sound becomes top-heavy. Conversely, if the other elements in the texture are not controlled, the sound can become cloudy when too many notes are played at an equal volume.

CLARITY AND THE RULE OF THREES

Intuition suggests a light thumb for the left hand in this Beethoven sonata second theme (fig. 5.1). Overplaying the B♭s will detract from the lyrical quality of the phrase with odd off-beat accents. Beethoven included them so that the eighth-note pattern creates a texture and rhythmic patter not otherwise possible, but these notes do nothing to add to the clarity of the overall harmonic structure. The left hand provides forward motion and keeps the phrase from bogging down. Because the phrase often consists of six notes in the left versus one note in the right hand, lightening up the thumb is crucial for allowing the long line of the right hand to be heard without interruption.

There is an even greater principle at work, though. The B♭s, other than adding to the rhythmic pulse, are subordinate to everything else in this section of the piece. If the melody commands chief attention and the moving notes of the bass line are a secondary interest, the B♭s are relegated to a fairly insignificant status. This compositional layering of three ideas is the most common texture found in piano music.

Humans are drawn to sets of threes, both visually and aurally. A "rule of threes" exists in art and photography and is in play on many levels in music. For example, ABA is the most common form in music. From simple folk tunes to sonata form (an extended ABA

(Allegro molto e con brio)

🎵 **FIG. 5.1** *mm. 56–63, Sonata in C Minor, op. 10, no. 1, I. Allegro molto e con brio, Beethoven*

composition), it permeates the repertoire with its clearly delineated three-part tempo-
ral structure. The rule of threes exists on a vertical level in music as well, with the vast
majority of homophonic music divisible in this way: the melody (first tier), a bass melody
(second tier), and everything else (third tier).

In the Beethoven sonata example, the first tier is the right-hand melody. The second tier comprises the left-hand notes that fall on each beat, which provide a counter-
melody to the right hand (fig. 5.2). Surprisingly, the combination of the bass melody
and the right-hand melody provides all of the harmonic information needed without
being informed by the B♭s. With just the outer voices, the harmonies are the same as
when the B♭s are added back in. Mapping these three tiers is demonstrated in figure
5.3. These can (and, in this case, must) have differing dynamics. The passage has a
written dynamic of piano, but this does not mean that every note is played piano. As
an example, the melody could land somewhere in the range of mezzo forte, the bass
melody at piano, and the repeated B♭s at pianissimo to create the overall impression
of piano (fig. 5.3).

ARE ALL OF THESE NOTES REALLY NECESSARY?

It is easy to spot the vertical division in this nocturne (fig. 5.4). The right hand features
the melody (first tier) and the lowest notes in the left hand supply a bass melody (second
tier). The middle slice of chords is the third tier. After separating out the bass clef, one can
see the melodic nature of the lowest bass line, followed by the C-C-F (V-V-I) cadence at
the end of the phrase (fig. 5.5).

As a general principle, the melodic line in the bass needs to be identified to provide
a counterbalancing force to the melody and to bring clarity to the texture as extraneous
notes are pushed to the background. With this adjustment, developing purposeful phrase

FIG. 5.2 *mm. 56–63, Sonata in C Minor, op. 10, no. 1, I. Allegro molto e con brio, Beethoven, bass melody*

FIG. 5.3 *mm. 56–63, Sonata in C Minor, op. 10, no. 1, I. Allegro molto e con brio, Beethoven, three tiers*

direction is much easier. The possibility for much longer pedals also begins to emerge because the accumulated sound buildup associated with the use of the damper pedal is lessened when fewer notes are voiced.

In this Chopin nocturne, the outline created by the melody and bass melodic line gives one a near perfect understanding of the harmonies, even withstanding the loss of the full chord. With just two voices, it is obvious that a third and possibly a fourth chord tone will be missing. Nevertheless, a listener will comprehend the proper harmonies in most cases. This is true in much of tonal music because certain expectations

FIG. 5.4 *mm. 1–8a, Nocturne in F Minor, op. 55, no. 1, Chopin*

(this line created by combining the chord-tone notes from tiers 1 and 2)

FIG. 5.5 *mm. 1–8a, Nocturne in F Minor, op. 55, no. 1, Chopin, bass melody*

have been set in place in regard to "what comes next" or at least what could come next. As in other aspects of life, ears take the path of least resistance and detect the most likely harmonies unless forced in a different direction. Leaving out the chords on beats two and four leads to the chord analysis found in figure 5.6. In the entire eight-bar phrase, one chord is ambiguous (m. 1) and one is misidentified (m. 6). On the first beat of measure one, the only question is whether the piece is in major or minor. The appearance of A♭ in the second-beat chord confirms that it is minor (fig. 5.7).

FIG. 5.6 *mm. 1–8a, Nocturne in F Minor, op. 55, no. 1, Chopin, harmonic analysis*

In measure six, the chord on beat four adds G♭, which changes it from the original analysis of B♭ minor to G♭ major (also, fig. 5.7). However, thirteen of fifteen chords were correctly identified by using only the melodic bass line and the melody. The ear will come to the same conclusion. This means that the chords on beats two and four throughout this passage can be minimized and pushed to the background using the softest dynamics possible without distressing the overall harmonies. If no dynamic sorting happens, major problems with clarity will be the result. If the entire left hand (bass line and chords) is played equally, the melody will be easily overpowered and lost as in the earlier Beethoven example. If all of the left hand is played at the same dynamic level and the melody is adjusted to compensate, the dynamic of piano is lost. Playing the chords as softly as possible allows for a depth in the softer dynamic range that is not possible any other way.

FIG. 5.7 *m. 1 and m. 6, Nocturne in F Minor, op. 55, no. 1, Chopin, harmonic analysis*

DOUBLE STEMMING

Sometimes, composers map the left-hand melody by using double-stemmed notes in the bass, as Schubert did in figure 5.8. This example differs from the previous two in that the right hand also contains third-tier material (fig. 5.9). For best voicing

FIG. 5.8 *mm. 1–5a, Sonata in A Major, D. 959, IV. Rondo, Schubert*

FIG. 5.9 *mm. 1–5a, Sonata in A Major, D. 959, IV. Rondo, Schubert, three tiers*

FIG. 5.10 *mm. 1–8a, Sonata in B♭ Major, op. 22, IV. Rondo, Beethoven*

FIG. 5.11 *mm. 1–8a, Sonata in B♭ Major, op. 22, IV. Rondo, Beethoven*

in pieces with three tiers, outer voices are weighted with louder dynamics while inner notes are deemphasized. In the Schubert sonata, if the right-hand notes are all played equally, the melodic line goes missing in a stream of overplayed chords. Bringing the top of the right hand out, in tandem with the double-stemmed notes in the left, allows the melodic phrase to be clearly heard, uninterrupted by heavy third-tier notes.

As in the previous example, Beethoven drew attention to the bass line using carefully detailed double stems (fig. 5.10). The rhythm in the bass melody is varied and imposes an inflection on the phrase that would be quite different if not for the use of the double stems. Beethoven crafted rhythmic elements in his music with particular detail. The bass melody is no exception, and using it as a rhythmic force greatly changes the landscape of this section (fig. 5.11).

ALBERTI BASS

One of the easiest bass melodies is found by stringing together the first notes of Alberti bass patterns. Some teachers even encourage students to "pedal" with the fifth finger by holding the first note of each set, which can be a nice gesture if not overdone. In this famous Mozart sonata, an Alberti bass is used to start the piece (fig. 5.12). As with other examples in this chapter, harmonies are fairly easy to determine without the third-tier notes (fig. 5.13). Although this bass melody is not particularly inspiring, it serves as a stabilizing element, counterbalancing the melody's disjunct motion and more intricate rhythm.

Similar is this Alberti bass example from a different Mozart sonata (fig. 5.14). Taking the elements apart, it is easy to see the bass melody (fig. 5.15). The harmonies are

FIG. 5.12 *mm. 1–4, Sonata in C Major, K. 545, I. Allegro, Mozart*

FIG. 5.13 *mm. 1–4, Sonata in C Major, K. 545, I. Allegro, Mozart, 1st and 2nd tiers*

FIG. 5.14 *mm. 1–4, Sonata in F Major, K. 332, II. Adagio, Mozart*

FIG. 5.15 *mm. 1–4, Sonata in F Major, K. 332, II. Adagio, Mozart, three tiers*

FIG. 5.16 *mm. 3–4, Sonata in F Major, K. 332, II. Adagio, Mozart, three tiers*

immediately apparent from just the outer voices, but what makes this example different lies in the third measure. Mozart alters the Alberti pattern by using just two different notes rather than the usual three, which results in a momentary stalling on E♭ and D. However, the third-tier notes suddenly break free into a moving line that creates contrary motion with the right hand (fig. 5.16).

Composers always shook things up to keep their music lively, so it is vital to make voicing and balancing choices at every step. Without having taken the bass apart for closer inspection, this treasure might have been missed. Here, it makes sense to briefly bring out the third-tier notes, but at the same dynamic level as the bass notes. Good taste should always be a consideration and thumping out off-beats under the melody at any point in a Mozart slow movement is probably not a good idea.

A FEW THOUGHTS ON OCTAVES

When both hands play the same notes in octaves, it is advisable to clearly voice the upper note. Since it is impossible to play both notes evenly, this keeps attention from shifting back and forth between them. In the opening of this Mozart sonata (fig. 5.17), voicing the right hand slightly keeps any left-hand notes from sticking out and hijacking the line (fig. 5.18).

Voicing becomes even more critical as the note values and tempos increase, as in this Beethoven sonata (fig. 5.19). Additionally, the lower the register used, the more important voicing becomes, unless the performer is after a growling, messy sound.

FIG. 5.17 *mm. 1–4a, Sonata in B♭ Major, K. 570, III. Rondo, Mozart*

FIG. 5.18 *mm. 1–4a, Sonata in B♭ Major, K. 570, III. Rondo, Mozart, suggested voicing*

FIG. 5.19 *mm. 30–39a, Sonata in G Major, op. 31, no. 1, I. Allegro vivace, Beethoven*

FIG. 5.20 *mm. 74b–78a, Sonata in G Major, op. 31, no. 1, III. Rondo: Allegretto, Beethoven*

When the left hand features broken octaves, as in this Beethoven sonata, a performer should consider playing the lower of the two notes louder (fig. 5.20). This allows the bass melody to come through without interference from the upper note. Again, this dynamic sorting affects rhythm by placing emphasis at the quarter note value.

POLYRHYTHMS AND VERTICAL SORTING

In almost every case, vertical sorting can clarify texture and is imperative when dealing with polyrhythms. As in the previous example, the bass in figure 5.21 should be voiced so the upper octave is played softly. In this particular section, doing so accomplishes a second goal of not allowing this rhythmically odd note to interfere with the right hand's triplet patterns.

Beethoven gives performers a little score advice for the polyrhythms found in the next sonata (fig. 5.22), with his use in the bass of double stems that visually reflect the

FIG. 5.21 *mm. 26–30a, Sonata in F Minor, op. 2, no. 1, III. Prestissimo, Beethoven*

FIG. 5.22 *mm. 31b–33, Sonata in F Major, op. 10, no. 2, I. Allegro, Beethoven*

FIG. 5.23 *mm. 32–33, Sonata in F Major, op. 10, no. 2, I. Allegro, Beethoven*

FIG. 5.24 *mm. 31b–33, Sonata in F Major, op. 10, no. 2, I. Allegro, Beethoven*

importance of the first note of each beat. In this section of the piece, only a few notes line up between the right and left hands. Attention should focus on the melody and the sextuplets in the bass should not interrupt. In the left hand, all but the first note of each beat should be played softly to avoid playing Ping-Pong with the melody (figs. 5.23 and 5.24). Although the rhythm should be exact, sadly, nobody is interested in hearing how much the twos against threes were practiced and perfected. Most of the notes of the left hand need to be deemphasized as shown in figure 5.24. It is important to figure out which notes are the interlopers and to relegate them to the lowest dynamic.

PEDAL POINTS

Pedal points are used by composers for varying effects and can provide a lulling bass, build tension, or simply imitate a drone instrument such as a bagpipe or hurdy gurdy. In this Mendelssohn work, the introduction has a typical bass line (fig. 5.25). These first six

FIG. 5.25 *mm. 1–7a, Venetianishes Gondelied in G Minor, op. 19, no. 6, Mendelssohn*

bars firmly establish the key and mood of the piece with only a few right-hand melodic notes attached, seemingly at random. In the measures that follow, Mendelssohn used a long pedal point in lieu of a bass melody. This type of bass line can have the effect of suspending a strong rhythmic impulse or the opposite, create tension with an unchanging and clashing bass line. In this case, Venetian Gondolier's Song, the pedal point possibly points to a slow, steady lapping of waves on the boat. If this is how a pianist understands it, these notes should not be suppressed in the texture. Bringing out the middle voices in this work could disrupt the character and mood of the piece, so voicing choices must be made thoughtfully. A significant moment occurs in measure fifteen when the pedal point G finally relents and moves to F, in preparation for the B section of the piece, which is free of pedal point (fig. 5.26). This transition should be brought forward and emphasized as it is both a dramatic and structural junction in the piece.

Unlike the Mendelssohn piece, the pedal point in this Beethoven rondo theme is nearly inconsequential except to recall the sound of the hurdy gurdy, a drone instrument. It does not create tension or dig against the harmonies of the piece. Here, a performer should consider bringing the middle voice forward in duet with the melody (fig. 5.27).

Understanding how a composer put together music for the left hand, particularly the writing of bass melodies, is essential for discovering balance between the vertical elements of a piece. There is almost always a chance to thin the texture and this winnowing process can lead to an ever-expanding dynamic and expressive range. With careful voicing, a performer can be the ultimate magician, bending an audience's ear toward particular notes or phrases. Also, subduing "unnecessary notes" by playing

FIG. 5.26 *mm. 7–19, Venetianishes Gondelied in G Minor, op. 19, no. 6, Mendelssohn, three tiers*

them quietly immediately expands the soft palate of expression allowing for a much wider spectrum of overall dynamics. Even though the emphasis here has been on developing three levels of interest, this textural treatment is one of many options. Voicing is just another spectrum to explore with a range that goes from bringing out just one note to playing all notes equally. At various times, either of these or something in between will be appropriate. Most of the time, however, performers will want to find clarity by weeding out the texture.

FIG. 5.27 *mm. 1–8a, Sonata in G Major, op. 31, no. 1, III. Rondo: Allegretto, Beethoven*

CHECKLIST FOR CHAPTER 5

- Is the score easily divided into three tiers?
  - Does the composer clearly outline a bass melody?
  - Are there double stems that make a bass line easier to identify?
  - Is the melodic rhythm slower than the accompaniment (i.e., hard to voice in a way that sustains the line)? If so, is there an easy way to thin the texture?
  - What notes or chords are least important and create the third tier?
  - Do the harmonies remain intact when leaving out the third tier? If not, what other notes need to be brought forward to make the harmonies clear?
- Is there an Alberti bass pattern?
  - If so, does the first note provide a clear bass melody that can be voiced?
  - Are there other aspects of the texture that might lead one to voice different notes for the bass melody?
- Are there octaves present?
  - How does this affect the voicing?
  - Which set of notes is subordinate?
- Are there polyrhythms (i.e., two against three)?
  - Which voice is subordinate?
  - What notes need to be played softly to keep the attention on the main melody?
- Is there a pedal point?
  - What is its purpose?
  - Does the pedal point heighten the tension of the phrase or lessen it?
  - Is the pedal point reminiscent of a drone instrument?

SIX

Messy Basses

OBSCURE BASS MELODIES

A bass melody cannot always be immediately identified from looking at a score and on analysis, several options may present themselves. A pianist must constantly judge whether the bass melody makes sense harmonically, rhythmically, and from the perspective of balance with the other elements above it.

Schumann's Hasche-Mann from *Kinderszenen* is a straightforward example that demonstrates the importance of harmonic analysis and melodies (fig. 6.1). Here, the bass melody provides the structural and harmonic muscle in an otherwise turbulent piece. Once the bass melody has been identified, the construction of the piece becomes clearer as the organization of the phrases start to leap from the page. The form is obviously ABA (mm. 1–8, mm. 9–16, and mm. 17–end), but on the surface the piece looks like it is much the same from beginning to end. However, with the bass melody defined, the contrasts between A and B become apparent. In the A section in B minor, bass melodic notes create strong underpinnings with their solid harmonic motion stemming from the fact that each note is the root of a primary chord in the key (i, iv, V^7). In the B section, this is not the case. Here, the piece moves through three key centers: G major, E minor, and C major. In the first two, the new "tonic" chords (although no modulation takes place) are inverted and weak. This, combined with the scant two bars given to each of these keys, leaves the section feeling unsettled. The piece then stalls out on a C major chord (♭II in the key of B minor, an exceptionally unusual choice) for two and a half measures. Even though the root is present in the bass, there is little going on here except a C major chord with fleeting references in the right hand to G^7. Coming straight out of this left-hand C drone bass is an F♯, a tritone away. The F♯^{7} chord leads immediately to the return of the A section. Because of this analysis, it is much easier to move forward with ideas on interpretation. An excellent way to mark bass melodies is by drawing in additional stems on the notes when a composer does not (fig. 6.2).

In a different way, Chopin uses the left hand in this nocturne to develop an engaging bass melody that often moves in stepwise motion and helps outline the overall harmonic structure (fig. 6.3). He ended the phrase by doubling the bass melody rhythm to a quarter-note bass pattern that steps down through the cadence (m. 9). Because of the steady and predictable bass line at the end of the phrase along with a quicker rhythmic pulse than earlier, the ritardando can be expanded greatly. Sorting out the bass melody in this piece accomplishes several tasks including making things sturdier for the rhythmically slow melody in the right hand. Secondly, focusing on just a few bass notes and playing the others very softly allows the melody a chance to be heard. Additionally, it keeps the polyrhythms (two against three in this passage) from sounding clumsy (fig. 6.4).

CHALLENGING BASS MELODIES

In this Brahms intermezzo, there are just two bass notes with double stems (mm. 4 and 8) in the first eight bars (fig. 6.5). Other signs appear to help a performer decide what the bass melody could be, but these are not immediately clear.

FIG. 6.1 (*Continued*)

FIG. 6.1 *Hasche-Mann from Kinderszenen, op. 15, R. Schumann*

FIG. 6.2 *mm. 1–4, Hasche-Mann from Kinderszenen, op. 15, R. Schumann, bass melody double stemmed*

The left hand bounces around, and choices must be made as to which notes to include and which to discard in determining a bass melody. When beginning to analyze a vague or muddy bass, it is helpful to look for V-I relationships between the lowest notes (rising fourths or descending fifths). With few exceptions, these should be considered as part

FIG. 6.3 *mm. 1–10a, Nocturne in E Minor, op. 72, no. 1, Chopin*

FIG. 6.4 *mm. 4–5, Nocturne in E Minor, op. 72, no. 1, Chopin*

FIG. 6.5 *mm. 1–8a, Intermezzo in A Major, op. 118, no. 2, Brahms*

FIG. 6.6 *mm. 3–4 and 7–8a, Intermezzo in A Major, op. 118, no. 2, Brahms*

of the bass melody. There are two that stand out in this example, both at phrase endings. Note that a V-I relationship does not mean V-I in any particular key, but rather it refers to the interval of a rising perfect fourth or falling perfect fifth between any two notes (fig. 6.6).

Otherwise, several options present themselves in the Brahms as they do in most pieces when determining a bass melody. Decisions on which notes to include should be made on a personal basis, of course, but with consideration of strong harmonic motion, recurring rhythmic patterns, motivic interest, and balance with the main melody.

In the Brahms, the left hand switches octaves several times. Compressing things into one octave for analytical purposes can be a helpful tool in measuring the value of each note. One interpretation can be found in figure 6.7 where the bass melody is written within a single octave. Several motivic and rhythmic elements make this example a viable option, such as an emphasis of a beat three to beat one pattern, along with points of stepwise motion. This also coordinates well with the melody, complementing it both rhythmically and harmonically (fig. 6.8).

FIG. 6.7 *mm. 1–8a, Intermezzo in A Major, op. 118, no. 2, Brahms, bass melody*

FIG. 6.8 *mm. 1–8a, Intermezzo in A Major, op. 118, no. 2, Brahms, outer voices*

As with the works from the previous chapter, the next steps are to assure that the harmonies are well represented by these two voices and, when they are not, to bring out other notes as necessary. With Brahms, the thick textures, combined with growling bass writing, provide the performer with an endless palette of colors. The spectrum runs from bringing out one note, voicing just the two notes in figure 6.8, or playing all notes equally. However, clarity is easily lost when careless voicing, especially in the bass, takes place. Using the same dynamic with all of the notes is effective for short periods of time when the piece merits it but is not a sustainable choice in Brahms.

TOO MANY NOTES

When the bass line comprises a steady stream of sixteenth notes, there are several options to consider. Should a performer bring out all of the notes, just the first note of each set, or something in between? In different passages, any of these could be a good answer. As seen earlier with the Alberti bass, it is usually sufficient to pull out the first note of each chord set. In this example from Beethoven, the bass pattern of six notes in a slow tempo could use a boost from the sixth note of each set (fig. 6.9). In this instance, the sixth note to the first often provides a V-I motion and even when they do not, the rhythm pushes the phrase forward to the next beat. Also, it alleviates the monotony of hearing just the E♭s, for example, at the start of each pattern and nothing more. The sixth notes in these sets

FIG. 6.9 *mm. 10–15, Sonata in G Major, op. 79, II. Andante, Beethoven*

should be played softer than the main bass notes, of course, but slightly louder than the other notes in the group. Attention to this detail, subtle as it may at first appear, clarifies the texture greatly and helps drive the music.

A similar example, but one in which the bass alone has the melody, is found in this Beethoven sonata (fig. 6.10). Playing all notes at the same dynamic and maintaining clarity would be difficult because of the speed and register of this passage. When this passage is analyzed, it is clear that Beethoven has simply dressed up a B♭ major chord, and it is these notes that propel this phrase.

CHOICES

There are times when many valid options present themselves, as in this Chopin nocturne (fig. 6.11). In pieces such as these, the best plan is to experiment and find a balance of

FIG. 6.10 *mm. 11b–13a, Sonata in B♭ Major, Op. 22, I. Allegro con brio, Beethoven*

FIG. 6.11 *mm. 1–9a, Nocturne in G Minor, op. 37, no. 1, Chopin*

notes that fits well with one's overall interpretation of the piece. Is it possible to hear the pattern in the first few measures of left-hand quarter notes as funereal wagon wheels of the funeral march from the third sonata? Although there is probably no direct tie between the opening and the B section of this work (a hymn like section written in quarter notes), bringing out all of the bass quarter notes for the first few measures certainly creates a connective rhythmic thread between the two parts. Can the audience detect this connection? Probably not, but it strengthens the overall structure of the piece nonetheless. The overall effect is a bass melody weak on melodic structures, but one that leans heavily

FIG. 6.12 *mm. 1–9a, Nocturne in G Minor, op. 37, no. 1, Chopin*

on rhythmic impulse instead (fig. 6.12). Bringing out the bass notes at the half-note level brings a completely different, but equally viable solution and one that has strong melodic components to it.

Spending the effort to plow through the myriad possibilities available to develop bass melodies is certainly worth the effort. It brings clarity to the texture, not just by the vertical resorting but also by making it possible to clearly trace the harmonic and rhythmic underpinnings of a work. Because the first-tier melody is usually defined by a composer and not up for debate, deciding on a bass melody and how it will interact with other elements is a creative detail that engages the personality of performers and differentiates performances.

CHECKLIST FOR CHAPTER 6

- When there is no obvious bass melody, what steps should be taken to find one?
- Are there other notes in the texture that would be helpful in defining harmonies?
  - Should these be added to the bass melody or just brought forward dynamically?
- Are there hard-to-see notes, such as those that are displaced by octaves that could be included in a bass melody?
- In a left-hand passage that contains a steady stream of notes, what elements help determine the bass melody?
  - Are there secondary notes that would help propel the line forward (perhaps the notes before the main bass notes)?
- Are there rhythmic elements that need to be considered in determining a bass melody?
  - Are there rhythmic elements that will favor one solution over another?

SEVEN

Ornamentation

Understanding the Small Print

ORNAMENTATION: A HORNET'S NEST

There are numerous books on the dos and don'ts of on-the-beat or off-the-beat advice regarding ornamentation, and some of them are referenced in the further reading at the end of this volume. This chapter will not take up the subject, and the best advice is to follow the rules explained in those sources, if possible. Here, the focus is less on performance practice and more on how to think through options for playing ornaments musically.

Common guidance for playing ornaments in Chopin is that they are an intrinsic, inseparable part of the overall melody. This approach also works for most ornamentation regardless of the composer or style. The reason usually given for the existence of any particular ornament is that it draws attention to the main note attached to it, which is a good place to start. Although there are exceptions to every rule, grace notes nearly always give energy to the note that follows. Most of the time, accenting the grace note, or even playing it at the same dynamic as the main note, throws the rhythm and phrasing off balance and sounds ugly and awkward. The same holds true for turns and most trills. As a benefit, observing this simple rule of not overemphasizing ornaments makes them much easier to play from a technical standpoint.

How fast, how loud, and where to play ornaments are major considerations. The character of a section of music, including its tempo and dynamics, has a direct impact on the performance of an ornament. For instance, the slower the tempo, the longer a grace note can be if it is not prescribed a preset length due to performance practice. As with other elements in interpretation, it is about keeping everything in context and within the boundaries of good taste.

ONE SMALL NOTE

Analyzing the lowly grace note can inform most other ornaments and, on a greater scale, melodic development. Questions to ask might include: Why did the composer write a grace note here? Is its purpose to give the performer flexibility in the rhythm? Does it indicate a likely rhythm that would be difficult to notate? Do notational conventions of the era point to a probable rhythm? Or could it simply enhance the main note, as in this Mendelssohn (fig. 7.1)? Should the fact that he used a thirty-second note value for this grace note bear any relationship to its performance? Possibly, but unless the sound of a squawking chicken is the desired effect, care should be taken to handle the grace note with, well, grace. Usually, with exceptions for those following particular performance practice protocols, the speed of a grace note should fall in line with the character of the surrounding passage.

Often, the rhythm given a grace note indicates the rhythm the composer wants, and in most cases, it is worthwhile to try it. In this section from his C Major Sonata, Haydn assigned a sixteenth note value to the grace notes, and it is appropriate to play them as such (fig. 7.2). In figure 7.3, the grace notes are written out as sixteenths, demonstrating the way they would be performed.

FIG. 7.1 *mm. 1–4a, Lied ohne Worte, op. 62, no. 1, Mendelssohn*

FIG. 7.2 *mm. 47–48, Sonata in C Major, Hob. XVI: 50, I. Allegro, Haydn*

FIG. 7.3 *mm. 47–48, Sonata in C Major, Hob. XVI: 50, I. Allegro, Haydn, grace notes written out*

FIG. 7.4 *mm. 47–48a, Sonata in C Major, Hob. XVI: 50, I. Allegro, Haydn, nonchord tones*

Students are quick to ask why Haydn did not just write this passage in sixteenth notes in the first place, if that was how he wanted it to sound. Mozart also used similarly "confusing" notation. On closer inspection, the grace notes are the nonchord tones of the group, and composers of this era are simply acknowledging the subordinate roles they play in the phrase by writing them the way they did. The main notes D, B, and G correspond to the G major chord in the bass clef, while grace notes E, C, and A do not (fig. 7.4). If Haydn had written out the notes as in figure 7.3, the grace notes would have been promoted in the tonal hierarchy. This does not mean that the chord tones should be accented, which would certainly sound awkward and out of place. It was simply a convention of the time to write this type of passage with grace notes.

Similarly, a grace note attached to a chord, such as in this Mozart sonata (fig. 7.5), could indicate an interpretation that utilizes the sixteenth note value indicated by the composer. The note associated with the grace note gets a late start, but the other notes should occur on the beat (fig. 7.6). The practice of using grace notes this way ended with

FIG. 7.5 *mm. 198–200a, Sonata in F Major, K. 332, III. Allegro assai, Mozart*

FIG. 7.6 *mm. 198–200a, Sonata in F Major, K. 332, III. Allegro assai, Mozart, grace note as performed*

Beethoven, who tended to write these sorts of passages with sixteenth notes regardless of any nonchord tone issues.

GRACE NOTES AND TRILLS

Occasionally, a grace note can clarify the dispute of whether a trill should start on the upper or main note, as demonstrated in measure nine of the mazurka in figure 7.7. Without it, the trill could start either on B or on the main note C. Here, Chopin made his wishes known by writing a grace note B just before the trill. In this case, the B starts the trill straight away on the beat. The fact that two Bs appear side by side does not mean that Chopin wanted a repeated note. It simply means that he had a strong opinion about the trill and its execution.

In the example, the two four-bar phrases are identical with the exception of the triplet versus the trill. By starting the trills on B in measures nine and eleven, the second phrase becomes a reflection of the first, in that both the triplets and the trills embrace the same basic note pattern (fig. 7.8).

(Allegro ma non troppo)

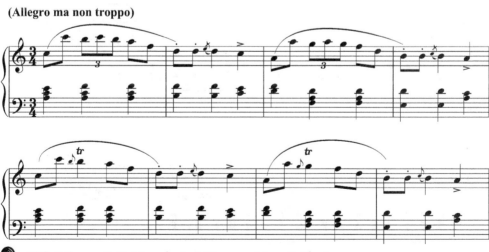

FIG. 7.7 *mm. 5–12, Mazurka in A Minor, op. 24, no. 2, Chopin*

FIG. 7.8 *mm. 5 and 9, Mazurka in A Minor, op. 24, no. 2, Chopin, trill written out for m. 9*

GRACE NOTES AND ORNAMENTS WITH
FLEXIBLE RHYTHMS

In certain instances, the use of grace notes can suggest a permissive rhythmic approach, especially in romantic music. This flexibility extends to both the grace note and the main note, as in this example from Chopin's E Minor Prelude (fig. 7.9). This grace note shows up just at the point at which the melodic line becomes more aggressive, giving the performer a chance to employ an agitated rhythm that fits the overall character of the phrase. Figure 7.10 shows one possible interpretation.

In this Bach sarabande, it is appropriate to play the ornaments in an improvisatory and melodic fashion considering their decorative nature and the slow tempo of the piece (fig. 7.11). Applying harsh rhythmic standards to the ornaments in this piece would destroy the beauty of the melody, and doing so is ill advised.

EDGY GRACE NOTES

What is purpose of the grace note in figure 7.12? If one did not know it was a Chopin mazurka, a gentle interpretation might prevail, especially considering the cantabile tempo

FIG. 7.9 *mm. 10–12, Prelude in E Minor, op. 28, no. 4, Chopin*

FIG. 7.10 *mm. 10–12, Prelude in E Minor, op. 28, no. 4, Chopin*

Sarabande

🔊 **FIG. 7.11** *mm. 1–4, Sarabande from French Suite no. 5 in G Major, BWV 816*

(Cantabile)

🔊 **FIG. 7.12** *mm. 17–20a, Mazurka in G Minor, op. 67, no. 2, Chopin*

marking. However, this passage comes later in the work, launching the rough-sounding B section. Here, this grace note is not at all graceful. In most music, grace notes hug their main note by a step and very few descend by a fourth as happens in this piece. This, combined with the disturbing underlying quartal harmony, should cue the performer that this is not a lyrical phrase. This grace note works well if given an ill-mannered, slightly comical treatment.

As exhibited in the last example, the distance between the grace note and main note plays a role in expression. In this nocturne, Chopin inserted a huge gap between the two (fig. 7.13). Generally, the larger the interval, the greater the amount of time one

(Andante)

🔊 **FIG. 7.13** *mm. 31–34a, Nocturne in E Minor, op. post. 72, no. 1, Chopin*

can take between the notes. Allowing for this extra time is necessary if the audience is to experience the leap and its distance with the performer. This also serves to keep the gesture from sounding like a musical hiccup, an easily generated, unintended side effect. The interval of the sixth at the beginning of figure 7.13 needs space, an easy task, but the grace note in the last measure of the example is tricky. The tenth (D♯-F♯) calls for time but not at the expense of breaking the melodic line from the preceding sextuplet to the F♯. Possibly, the best solution is to make a ritardando during the sextuplets to allow enough time for the grace note and for the melody to bridge the gap.

TURNS

In the opening of this Mozart second movement, the melodic line unfolds with a sequence of turns (fig. 7.14). Several different rhythmic treatments of these ornaments will work, but the main interest here is in how to play them musically.

Making the first note of any turn the softest and playing a crescendo to the main note always works (fig. 7.15). Not only is it easier to play, it allows all notes to be heard. If the first note is louder than the ones that follow, these subsequent notes will be lost and the sound of the turn will be muddy. Keeping the first note unaccented pushes the energy through every note of the turn. The goal, after all, is to draw interest to the main note. Additionally, from a technical standpoint, starting an ornament by "grinding it into the keybed" will ensure that the fingers will get stuck with excess tension, which would leave them unable to move well enough to play the rest of the notes. This technique of playing the first note softly and making a crescendo to the main note works with most multiple-note ornaments as well.

FIG. 7.14 *mm. 1–2, Sonata in F Major, K. 332, II. Adagio, Mozart*

FIG. 7.15 *mm. 1–2, Sonata in F Major, K. 332, II. Adagio, Mozart*

TRILLS VERSUS TURNS

When played, written turns and trills often sound exactly alike, and in some instances, their symbols are interchangeable. A trill can be as short as three notes if started from the main note and as short as four notes if started on the upper, unwritten note. Of course, a trill is improvisatory in that it can have as many beats (or sets of two notes) as possible or at least as many as one can play in good taste. This is not the case with turns where the only choice is whether to start on the upper or main note, and even this is not always an option. Turns can be written out, as in the Mozart example, appear as trills with tails, or sometimes as just the symbol ∾. Some trills have no tail notes attached, but it sounds right to add them. There are often many choices available to the performer when executing these ornaments. Figures 7.16 through 7.18 demonstrate some of the possibilities (rhythms may vary).

Usually, accommodating a tail at the end of a trill takes on one of two rhythms. If the trill begins on the upper note, the tail notes should spin out in the same rhythm. It is a different matter when the trill begins on the main note, however. An adjustment by a triplet just before the tail notes makes the trill rhythmically viable (fig. 7.19). This is an example of a measured trill, one where the beats are played according to a rigorous rhythmic pattern.

FIG. 7.16 *A few trill performance possibilities*

FIG. 7.17 *Turn performance possibilities*

FIG. 7.18 *Turn and trill interpreted in the same way*

(**Allegro maestoso**)

FIG. 7.19 *mm. 120–121a, Sonata in A Minor, K. 310, I. Allegro maestoso, Mozart, trill written out*

Compositions with a strong, rhythmic pulse, like those in faster works by Bach, benefit from measured trills, such as this invention (fig. 7.10). Here, the right-hand trill is played with notes twice as fast as those in the bass. Since the trill starts on the upper note, there is no need to add a triplet toward the end.

Three different-looking turns and trills from this Beethoven sonata appear within three pages of one another, but each has a different interpretive outcome. (figs. 7.21, 7.22, and 7.23).

The obvious visual differences in the figures raise questions of how this might affect the way they sound. The first example falls within the first theme group, which is heavily rhythmic. It may be that Beethoven wanted the tail of the trill played exactly, in thirty-second notes, so he wrote out that particular rhythm (fig. 7.24).

FIG. 7.20 *mm. 18–22, Invention in D Minor, BWV 775, J. S. Bach*

FIG. 7.21 *mm. 21–21, Sonata in C Major, op. 2, no. 3, I. Allegro con brio, Beethoven*

FIG. 7.22 *mm. 27–28, Sonata in C Major, op. 2, no. 3, I. Allegro con brio, Beethoven*

FIG. 7.23 *mm. 81b–83, Sonata in C Major, op. 2, no. 3, I. Allegro con brio, Beethoven*

FIG. 7.24 *mm. 21–22b, Sonata in C Major, op. 2, no. 3, I. Allegro con brio, Beethoven, one trill option*

FIG. 7.25 *mm. 27–28a, Sonata in C Major, op. 2, no. 3, I. Allegro con brio, Beethoven*

FIG. 7.26 *mm. 81b–83, Sonata in C Major, op. 2, no. 3, I. Allegro con brio, Beethoven, first note of trill emphasized for overall direction and attention to rhythm and energy of the line*

The second example is more lyrical in nature and does not need a careful rhythmic treatment of the turn. Figure 7.25 shows one option for playing this, although the execution of the ornament can have a messier rhythm than shown.

The third example could be interpreted the same as a turn (four notes plus the following quarter note for each one), but to do so would fail the character of the moment, which simply calls for more notes. Most likely, the passage should have all the "charm of a coffee grinder" as it fights its way to the closing theme.

THE FULL GESTURE OF A TRILL

Discovering where a trill truly starts and ends is also crucial, as there may be notes leading up to and away from the marked trill that should be included in the overall musical gesture. In the Mozart example found in figure 7.27, the first trill should include the upbeat G, the trill itself, two tail notes, and a resolution note as bracketed in the first measure of the example. The second is similar, but the tail notes are written as grace notes rather than

FIG. 7.27 *mm. 16b–19a, Sonata in F Major, K. 332, II. Adagio, Mozart*

in actual note values. The upbeats for each should be played softer than the first note of the trill, and a decrescendo should accompany the last three notes for the passage to be heard as one musical gesture.

Obviously, the ornaments in this chapter represent only a tiny fraction of those in the literature, but these examples point to a healthy attitude towards analyzing and developing ornaments of all varieties. Although there are almost no comments in regard to performance practice, the rules that apply to various periods of music and those for specific composers cannot be ignored.

CHECKLIST FOR CHAPTER 7

- General
  - Why did the composer choose to write an ornament in a particular place?
  - What was the composer trying to communicate?
  - What is the purpose of the ornament?
- Grace Notes
  - What is the value given the grace note by the composer?
  - Is the rhythm of an ornament rigid or flexible?
  - Are there performance practices that would inform the way you should play a grace note? Are grace notes parts of, for example, a sixteenth note passage? Should a grace note start on the beat or before the beat?
  - Is the grace note expressive or rhythmic?
  - Does the tempo of the piece affect the speed of the grace note?
  - How could small-scale dynamics help shape the ornament?
  - Should an ornament match or mimic another melodic figure found nearby?
  - Should the ornament be lyrical, rhythmic, or aggressive in nature?
- Turns and Trills
  - How can small-scale dynamics help the execution and clarity of an ornament?
  - Should a turn or trill start on the main or upper note?
  - Should a trill be played in a measured way (played in a specific rhythm)?
  - Does the trill sound better with a tail? Would it be appropriate to add one?
- More general questions
  - Is there more than one way to interpret an ornament? If so, which one fits best with the passage?
  - What is the full ornament? Are there notes ahead or after the ornament that should be included in the overall gesture?

EIGHT

Rubato

Stealing as an Art

RUBATO: FACT AND FICTION

Although seldom indicated in a score, rubato should be the constant companion of every piece. Unfortunately, much of what performers claim to be rubato is just bad timing that communicates nothing more than chaos to the listener. Freedom in expression is expansive, but only within the parameters of good taste appropriate for each compositional era and work. Although there are a few specific exceptions, rhythm should not break the structures that hold it, even when bent. When rubato is marked in a score, *a piacere, espressivo, ad libitum, senza tempo,* as well as *rubato* are all composer blessings on rhythmic liberties.

Several misconceptions need to be set aside before a discussion of what works can begin. One is that rubato is for use mainly in the romantic era. On some level, performers flex rhythm in every piece for expressive purposes, and it is impossible to play a piece without it. The best harpsichordists play with a creative rubato that often translates aurally as dynamics. Rubato and Bach? Yes![1]

Another concept is that rubato for some composers should spring from a steady and unbending left hand and a meandering right hand. While this is certainly an occasional option, it does not work effectively for most music.

Thirdly, a few ethically minded musicians argue that if you steal time, you must give it back. Since the definition of stealing does not include giving back the things that were

---

[1] See Paul Badura-Skoda, *Interpreting Bach at the Keyboard* (Oxford: Oxford University Press, 2002), for several discussions on Bach and rubato.

stolen, this may not be a good idea if it means one is doing so out of a sense of obligation rather than for musical reasons. Rubato occasionally calls for accelerandos, but the use of these is very specific and should be carefully executed.

GENERAL PRINCIPLES

The secret to developing strong instincts in rubato is multifold. First, the performer must decide what effect he or she is trying to achieve with each phrase. Is there a surprise, such as a deceptive cadence, that needs emphasis? Is there a call to create a smooth bridge from one phrase to the next? Are there leaps or interesting rhythms that would benefit from some rhythmic wiggle room? Is there a note or chord that needs extra attention?

A performer must constantly juggle being in three places at all times: knowing where the music has been, how it relates to the present, and planning where things are heading. The most important is the ability to work ahead, predicting where the music is going and making adjustments to create the space for it to happen. With forethought and planning, rhythm can bend to a tremendous degree without disturbing the overall structure. When rhythm adjusts to allow an event to become extraordinary, the audience experiences the music as it takes place instead of afterwards when they might wonder, "What was that?"

Regardless of the era, composer, or tonality, there are always pushes and pulls in music that need to be expressed rhythmically. Although rubato reflects one of the most deeply personal expressions in music, developing a repertoire of what works and what does not and having many possibilities at one's fingertips at all times keep performances fresh and alive.

RUBATO BETWEEN PHRASES

When ending a large section of a work, such as the end of a development section within sonata form, it works well to make a ritardando following the guidelines found in chapter 3 for ending a piece. Often, the new section can start *a tempo* without any tempo transition because the strength of the architecture can withstand the jolt. In such cases, composers frequently write a fermata or long rest to indicate the separation of the two sections, such as in the junction between the development section and recapitulation in this sonata by Beethoven (fig. 8.1). The *a tempo* can start immediately on beat four after the fermata.

However, smaller sections and phrases within larger forms are structurally much weaker and normally cannot endure sudden changes of tempo. These call for natural-sounding transitions using rubato to bridge phrases, created by using both a

FIG. 8.1 *mm. 124–127 Sonata in B♭ Major, op. 22, I. Allegro con brio, Beethoven*

ritardando and short accelerando. For example, when a composer writes an *a tempo*, it is usually at a place where the music needs to begin heading back to the original tempo and not the place where the *a tempo* actually starts. When the main theme returns in Chopin's first nocturne, the *a tempo* needs to start somewhere after the barline and not at the barline (fig. 8.2). The ritardando should follow through across the barline and into the first beat of the *a tempo* measure. Then, a short accelerando beginning with the second eighth note should continue until somewhere between beats three and four before it dovetails back into the prevailing tempo (fig. 8.3). Note that the rallentando covers quite a bit more territory than the accelerando does. Generally, a short accelerando is sufficient, and actually desirable, for moving the piece back to *a tempo*.

Deciding where to begin a back-to-tempo accelerando is one of two crucial elements in making smooth transitions between phrases. The other is figuring out where to begin the *a tempo* so it sounds natural. Although composers most often place an *a tempo* marking at the beginning of the new measure, starting it there is usually a bad idea.

FIG. 8.2 *mm. 69–71, Nocturne in B♭ Minor, op. 9, no. 1, Chopin*

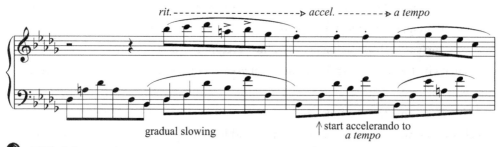

FIG. 8.3 *mm. 70–71, Nocturne in B♭ Minor, op. 9, no. 1, Chopin,* a tempo *starts on beat three*

FIG. 8.4 *mm. 42–44, Sonata in B♭ Major, op. 22, I. Allegro con brio, Beethoven*

FIG. 8.5 *mm. 42b–44, Sonata in B♭ Major, op. 22, I. Allegro con brio, Beethoven*

Quite often, phrases resolve on the downbeat of a measure, so particular care must be taken to follow a ritardando into the next measure and through the full completion of the phrase. In this Beethoven sonata, the melodic line is G–F–E–D–C–B♭–A. Likewise, the other voices descend downward, all resolving on the downbeat of measure forty-four (fig. 8.4). The accelerando begins quickly afterwards and pulls the new phrase up to tempo.

When a piece dramatically shifts character from one measure to the next, a slight ritardando and accelerando provide an effective transition. In this Beethoven example (fig. 8.5), it would be possible to play without any fluctuation in tempo, but some give and take guide the listener through the changes as they occur.

Composers sometimes use an accompanimental figure to bridge phrases. In the famous second movement of the Pathétique Sonata, triplets connect the end of one phrase to the beginning of the next (fig. 8.6). The triplets do not really "belong" to either phrase but stand in the gap between them. Here, the ritardando works best when it stretches into beat two of measure eight. Following is an accelerando beginning on the E♭ in the third beat, which moves through the barline to the first event of measure nine. If the ritardando extends into the *a tempo*, the phrase becomes intolerably slow, so using the triplets to get back up to speed works well in this situation. Additionally, one should plan the rubato carefully so the triplets are actually heard as triplets. It is a bit of an awkward spot for Beethoven to have introduced a new rhythmic impulse (duplets to triplets), but it is possible to play it effectively without undermining the beat. This harmonically static area only serves to lift the theme to a new octave, and playing an accelerando gives momentum to an otherwise dull arpeggio.

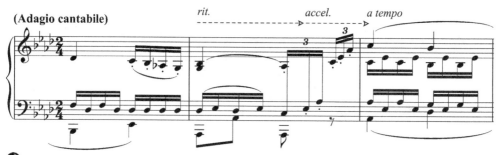

FIG. 8.6 *mm. 7–9, Sonata in C Minor, op. 13, II. Adagio cantabile, Beethoven*

ELIDED PHRASES

In the Mozart sonata in figure 8.7, it is important for the ritardando to go all the way to the beginning of the next phrase as with previous examples. On closer inspection, though, it is clear that the note finishing the first phrase also begins the next (fig. 8.8). These elided phrases are possibly the trickiest types of phrase junctures to execute effectively, and gauging the timing of the ritardando and accelerando into *a tempo* is more delicate than in other types of phrase alignments.

In the first movement of this same sonata, Mozart strung several elided phrases together to create a superphrase of twelve bars (fig. 8.9). Slight nods to the smaller phrase endings through tiny ritardando/accelerando pairings can help create a beautiful opening to the work, but overdoing the effect might cause the audience to feel unsettled. Additionally, the use of small-scale dynamics can help smooth transitions between phrases. Pianists know to use a decrescendo at the end of a phrase so that the last note is the softest, unless otherwise marked. This remains true for elided phrases, even though the last note is also

FIG. 8.7 *mm. 4–5, Sonata in F Major, K. 332, II. Adagio, Mozart*

FIG. 8.8 *mm. 4–5, Sonata in F Major, K. 332, II. Adagio, Mozart*

FIG. 8.9 *mm. 1–12a, Sonata in F Major, K. 332, I. Allegro, Mozart, dynamics added*

the first note of the next phrase. At this point, a crescendo can bring the piece back up to the overall dynamic, but that process must not start until after the resolving note.

In some works, the accompaniment moves at a quicker pace than the melody. In this Schubert impromptu, the underlying right-hand sextuplets must manage the rubato between phrases and not the upper, slow-moving melody (fig. 8.10). Organizing the rhythmic impulse of a rubato simply depends on the fastest moving notes of a phrase.

FIG. 8.10 *mm. 1–5a, Impromptu in G♭ Major, op. 90, no. 3, Schubert*

RHYTHMIC CONSIDERATIONS

Composers sometimes include rhythmic gestures that make developing effective rubatos challenging. In this Beethoven sonata, measure twenty-five stalls out with single eighth notes, creating a substantial foil to the preceding measure's relatively complex rhythms (fig. 8.11). These eighths serve to stabilize the rhythm, so a ritardando (if any) belongs at the end of the measure with minimum flex in the tempo. Here, these notes provide a cushioning bridge between the two phrases. Measure twenty-six, while it should start a little late as a follow through of the ritardando, should start *a tempo*. It is an exception to the rule, of course, showing that it is not possible to apply a standard rubato to all phrase connections. When rhythmic values are mixed, as in this one, it may be that a rubato cannot stretch quite as widely as in places where rhythm is more static.

This mazurka expresses a different rhythmic dilemma where Chopin wrote a poco ritardando in an impractical place (fig. 8.12). If a ritardando starts with beat one of this measure, there would be no clear way of distinguishing the two eighths from the dotted eighth/sixteenth that dominates most of the rest of piece. Something would sound very wrong. Pushing the start of the ritardando into the next bar makes far better sense and allows for clarity in the change of rhythm in the preceding measure (fig. 8.13).

FIG. 8.11 *mm. 24–26, Sonata in G Major, op. 14, no. 2, I. Allegro, Beethoven*

FIG. 8.12 *mm. 197–203a, Mazurka in B Minor, op. 33, no. 4, Chopin*

FIG. 8.13 *mm. 197–203a, Mazurka in B Minor, op. 33, no. 4, Chopin*

🔊 **FIG. 8.14** *mm.10b–13, Sonata in C Minor, op. 10, no. 1, III. Finale: Prestissimo, Beethoven*

There are many occasions when composers (and Beethoven, in particular) intentionally created a musical jolt when rhythm, character, and/or dynamics change without warning. In this sonata, the rhythmic impulse of the melody doubles from one phrase to the next as it takes off in wild scalar passagework (fig. 8.14). In situations in which an unexpected surprise takes the piece in a sudden change of direction, an *a tempo* directly at the new phrase can work effectively to highlight the contrast. If used here, the drama of this junction is greatly heightened. Taking the character of two colliding passages into consideration is paramount when developing ideas around rubato.

AGOGIC ACCENTS

Figures 8.15 and 8.16, one from Haydn and the other from Beethoven, contain passages that seem to get stuck and spin around without direction. There are no clues as to when they might turn a corner and do something different. Both could benefit from an agogic accent at the point at which they finally end their repetitive patterns, as a signal that things are finally breaking in a new direction. There are several definitions of agogic accents, but only one is used in this chapter, indicating an accent of time created by delaying certain notes. These accents are tricky and can be ineffective if a note or chord is played so late that the overall rhythmic structure is destroyed, so good timing is crucial.

A successful way to communicate to an audience that a moment is special is through these delaying tactics. The pause, even though it is just a fraction of a second, creates anticipation in the listener and signals that the next note or chord is important. Pushing the tempo and rushing into a new phrase may feel exciting for the performer, but most of the time it is far from electrifying for the audience.

(Allegro)

FIG. 8.15 *mm. 10b–15a, Sonata in C Major, Hob. XVI: 50, I. Allegro, Haydn, legato should continue past the wedge to the E*

(Prestissimo)

FIG. 8.16 *mm. 13–22a, Sonata in F Minor, op. 2, no. 1, IV. Prestissimo, Beethoven*

🔊 **FIG. 8.17** *mm. 3–4a, Nocturne in E♭ Major, op. 9, no. 2, Chopin*

🔊 **FIG. 8.18** *mm. 36–43, Sonata in C Minor, K. 467, I. Allegro, Mozart*

Another place that an agogic accent works well is where the melodic line suddenly takes a leap, as in this Chopin nocturne (fig. 8.17). Although the delay is short, it is sufficient for the audience to switch registers along with the performer. The bonus is that one has extra time to make the jump, which is particularly useful in fast passagework or leaping grace notes.

Similarly, an agogic accent is valuable when a melody changes registers. Again, slightly delaying the first note of a melody that suddenly flies out of range signals to a listener to pay closer attention. In this Mozart sonata, the melody shifts from hand to hand and from octave to octave. Using agogic accents to make the leaps creates more clarity than if the new phrase arrives on time (fig. 8.18). Once the ear is used to the ongoing register swings, agogic accents are no longer useful and can become predictable and cloying.

Likewise, the rising sixths and sevenths that lift the theme to new registers in the fantasy section of this Bach prelude could benefit from a sliver of extra time (fig. 8.19).

DYNAMIC ACCENTS

sf or *sfz* markings can also be interpreted as agogic accents rather than, or in addition to, dynamic ones. Delaying the chords in this Beethoven sonata, combined with a slight

🔊   **FIG. 8.19**   *mm. 1–3, Prelude and Fugue in E♭ Major, W.T.C. I, BWV 852, Prelude, J. S. Bach*

FIG. 8.20   *mm. 20–24, Sonata in F Minor, op. 2, no. 1, I. Allegro, Beethoven*

dynamic accent creates a more compelling line than if only dynamic accents were used (fig. 8.20). *sf* accents should be played in context with the prevailing dynamic indication. Here, Beethoven placed them in a phrase marked *p*, so the accents should not be overly loud.

An agogic accent is also useful when dynamics shift suddenly from loud to soft, as with an *fp* or simply with a change to *p* after a long crescendo as in this Beethoven scherzo (fig. 8.21). This minor delay gives the heavier dynamic more time to dissipate, allowing the softer notes a better chance to be heard as the new theme appears.

🔊   **FIG. 8.21**   *mm. 78–84, Sonata in E♭ Major, op. 31, no. 3, II. Scherzo: Allegretto vivace, Beethoven*

(Allegro con brio)

FIG. 8.22 *mm. 28–31, Sonata in D Major, Hob. XVI: 37, I. Allegro con brio, Haydn*

DECEPTIVE CADENCES AND AGOGIC ACCENTS

In figure 8.21, the C major chord in measure eighty-three is unexpected. This new phrase should have been in C minor according to the expectations set by the harmonies of the preceding measures. Although deceptive cadences are often described as having a V-vi motion, any move at a cadential point to a surprise harmony may be considered deceptive, as in this example.

Haydn, in his comical way, spun through several key areas in sixteenth notes and still managed to surprise the listener with the B♭ major chord that lands in measure thirty (fig. 8.22). An agogic accent is useful at deceptive cadences, because the delay will highlight the harmonic twist for the audience.

GRAVITY, MUSIC, HANG TIME, AND SLINGSHOTS

The high B in this Chopin nocturne arrives only after the great effort of leaping all the way up from the G on beat one (fig. 8.23). It is as if gravity tugs on this phrase on the way up and then pulls the whole thing back down again after the high point is reached, which can be played effectively by using a ritardando/accelerando pairing (fig. 8.24).

Feeling the gravitational pull of a melodic line is often the key to making it come alive. Many try to play this famous scale from Chopin's Nocturne in C♯ Minor exactly in rhythm and tempo (fig. 8.25). This is impossible for most pianists to accomplish and sounds out of place when they can.

When a basketball player jumps to make a shot, there is a moment when he or she seems suspended in midair before coming back down. The term for this point when the

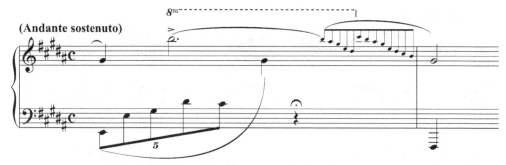

FIG. 8.23 *mm. 60–61a, Nocturne in B Major, op. 32, no. 1, Chopin*

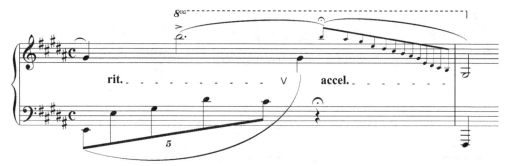

FIG. 8.24 *mm. 60–61a, Nocturne in B Major, op. 32, no 1, Chopin*

FIG. 8.25 *mm. 59–60a, Nocturne in C♯ Minor, op post., Chopin*

upward energy of the jumper can no longer escape gravity and momentum begins to shift downwards, is *hang time*. This energy is useful in melodic phrases as well and is represented in the next examples by a short fermata (𝕒). In the Chopin nocturne (fig. 8.26), tremendous energy pushes the scale upward, hang time catches the D♯ at the top, and gravity pulls the scale downward. This treatment of the scale sounds far better than simply trying to play it evenly.

Hang time grabs the phrase in Chopin's Waltz in A♭ Major in a different way. The first four notes of this phrase wind up like an old-fashioned slingshot, fling the rest of the grace note run upward to the G♭ and over into the rest (fig. 8.27). To play this effectively, a short accelerando needs to push from the second A to the G♭ as shown

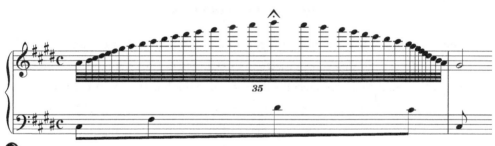

FIG. 8.26 *mm. 59–60a, Nocturne in C♯ Minor, op. post., Chopin*

FIG. 8.27 *mm. 26–28, Waltz in A♭ Major, op. 69, no. 1, Chopin*

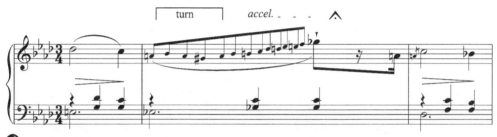

FIG. 8.28 *mm. 26–28, Waltz in A♭ Major, op. 69, no. 1, Chopin*

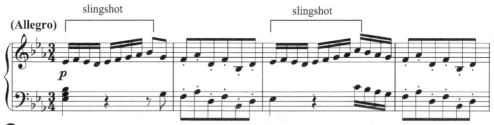

FIG. 8.29 *mm. 25–28, Sonata in E♭ Major, op. 31, no. 3, I. Allegro Beethoven*

in figure 8.28. Here, hang time catches during the rest and not at the top note of the phrase.

The slingshot effect shows up in many different forms, often as a written-out turns, and the energy of this windup is effective in pushing the phrase forward, as in this phrase by Beethoven (fig. 8.29). The second turn throws the phrase just a step further than the first and may be played more emphatically.

ROLLER COASTERS?

Although it may sound irreverent, the rubato developed for a phrase can resemble the rises and falls of a ride on a roller coaster. In this Chopin nocturne, it is not difficult to see how gravity could positively affect the interpretation this line (figs. 8.30 and 8.31).

Playing this Beethoven phrase faithfully to a roller coaster outline would sound overdone and inappropriate, but the energy of the line is worth adopting at some level (fig. 8.32). Without feeling the pushes and pulls that gravity suggests, a line like this would be meaningless and dull.

FIG. 8.30 *mm. 12–14, Nocturne in F♯ Major, op. 15, no. 2, Chopin*

FIG. 8.31 *mm. 12–14, Nocturne in F♯ Major, op. 15, no. 2, Chopin*

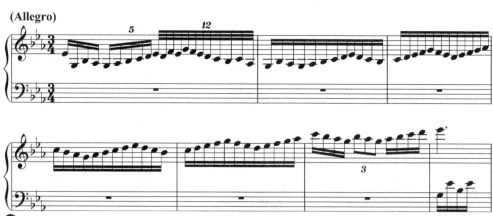

FIG. 8.32 *mm. 177–183a, Sonata in E♭ Major, op. 31, no. 3, I. Allegro, Beethoven*

Likewise, for the ending of this Chopin nocturne, gravity and motion must inform the rubato (fig. 8.33). Much as leaves defy falling straight to the ground, this phrase is the downward pull of gravity combined with the occasional uplift of the line to another level (fig. 8.34). This gentle rubato allows the repetitious motifs to have direction and breath.

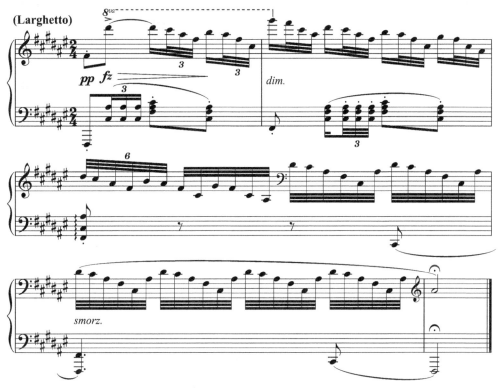

FIG. 8.33 *mm. 58–62, Nocturne in F♯ Major, op. 15, no. 2, Chopin*

FIG. 8.34 *mm. 58–60a, Nocturne in F♯ Major, op. 15, no. 2, Chopin*

Rubato is probably the most intimate of all individual expressions and its use and breadth define a performer. Traditionally, this element of music has been left to chance and to a performer's inner feelings, but perhaps finding rubato can include analysis in addition to these subjective factors. Ultimately, its successful interpretation lies in striking the right balance between performance practice, an ability to manipulate rhythm, and the personal conviction of how a piece should be performed.

CHECKLIST FOR CHAPTER 8

- How can the folklore around rubato negatively affect the piece or passage at hand?
- Is there a need for rubato at this point in the music?
  - Perhaps no rubato is needed:
    At the beginning of most pieces (from chapter 2).
    At a major intersection in a piece.
    After a fermata, especially one on a rest.
- What should one do at phrase seams?
  - Is there an *a tempo* indicated?
  - If so, where is the end of the phrase coming into the *a tempo*?
  - Is the ritardando continuing to this point?
  - Should the *a tempo* start later than indicated in the score? If so, where exactly?
  - Where should the accelerando start? Does it dovetail into the *a tempo* effectively?
  - If there is no *a tempo*, is this a place that could benefit from a ritardando/accelerando?
  - If so, where does the first phrase end and where does the second phrase begin?
  - Are the phrases elided?
  - Does the rubato move naturally between the two phrases?
  - Is it necessary to employ the accompaniment as the main driver of a ritardando/accelerando?
  - Is there an accompanimental figure that bridges two phrases?
  - How can dynamics help things move more smoothly?
- Are there problematic rhythms that demand extra planning when considering rubato?
- Would it be appropriate to use an agogic accent?
  - Are there repetitive subphrases that suddenly let loose in a different direction?
  - Is there an unexpected or special note or chord?
  - Are there *sf*, *sfz*, *fp*, or other dramatic dynamic marks?
  - Is there a sudden change of dynamic?
  - Is there a cadence that does not resolve as expected (deceptive cadence)?
- How does gravitational pull affect a melodic line?
  - Where is the top of a phrase?
  - Would hang time shape a line better?
  - Are there leaps?
  - Would a "slingshot" effect be useful and interesting?
  - Are there special shapes to the line that might indicate how rubato might work best?

NINE

Deconstructing Phrases

MEANING IN EVERY MELODIC NOTE

Most written music has slur markings, so why engage in a conversation about phrasing? Why not just follow what the composer indicated? Unfortunately, most composers give few clues as to their intentions in regard to phrasing, even when they use slur marks. If used at all, slurs can signal a wide variety of meanings. Yes, they can indicate phrase structure but just as often inform articulation. Some composers also use slurs in a negative way, as to say, "Do not break this set of notes apart." However, the notes that occur before and after these slur marks are not necessarily excluded from the phrases. Markings such as slurs, articulation, rests, and dynamics simply do not define the phrase as a whole. For pianists in particular, slurs are difficult to trust, and it is often problematic to determine exactly what they should mean to one's playing. A performer must try to understand the intentions of a given composer for a given piece and for a given phrase and give up on the idea of faithfully following slurs as phrase markings. Of course, one still needs to decide how long each phrase will last. Once determined, the apex is, more often than not, the turning point dynamically within a given phrase. But, at a level below this, the ultimate discovery is how the phrases are put together in the first place with small, usually two- to four-note subphrases that shape melody. Chapter 4 began this discussion with a look at what notes belong together rhythmically, but this is not the only factor that joins notes together into subphrases. Rhythm can often trump melodic factors, and harmony ultimately affects melodic tension. All three elements work in tandem to create forces of tension and resolution and must be taken into account as a team when determining subphrases.

As is common practice, a performer generally makes a decrescendo at the end of a phrase. There is a dynamic lean on the notes and chords that create tension and a feeling of relaxation brought to those things that convey resolution. This relationship between tension and resolution exists in every piece, and it is the performer's obligation to bring this out. At the simplest core, one plays them all the same way: Tension is louder, and resolution is softer unless otherwise marked, whether in Mozart or Prokofiev. Instead of relegating this practice only to phrase endings, extending it into the subphrases can bring meaning to every note of a melody as well as give a performer the option of spinning out a phrase indefinitely.

Revisiting an example by Mozart from chapter 4 is a good place to start to understand the value of finding and developing subphrases, especially since he does a good job at hiding them. He is a composer in the "do not break this set of notes apart" category. The slur marks here might lead one to think that the phrases start at the beginning of each measure and end at the barlines (fig. 9.1). Although some argue that Mozart intended to affect articulation with this type of slur, this does not mean that it makes musical sense to separate the phrase in such a way on a modern instrument. However, the notes that appear at the ends of slur marks either musically lead to the next phrase or actually end the phrase, so a dynamic dip is appropriate and probably necessary.

If Mozart had not included phrase markings, the following interpretation might be the result, with the same groupings identified in chapter 4 as belonging together both musically and rhythmically (fig. 9.2). Mozart's original slurs immediately rule out this possibility, though. Conversely, the phrases outlined in figure 9.2 make sense, so how does one justify the two? If the "do not break these notes apart" slurs do not exclude the notes around them, combining these two ideas becomes a possibility. Putting these two sets of slurs together creates a complete four-bar phrase (figs. 9.3 and 9.4). Some editions simply provide the phrasing found in figure 9.4, disregarding the original slurs. The two-note groupings that cross the barline are the subphrases that generate the energy necessary to propel the music forward. Even though Mozart did not mark them, it is necessary to acknowledge these small connections to create a breathing, energized interpretation

FIG. 9.1 *mm. 1–5, Sonata in F Major, K. 332, I. Allegro, Mozart*

FIG. 9.2 *mm. 1–5a, Sonata in F Major, K. 332, I. Allegro, Mozart*

FIG. 9.3 *mm. 1–5a, Sonata in F Major, K. 332 I. Allegro, Mozart, combined phrasing*

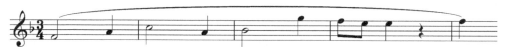

FIG. 9.4 *mm. 1–5a, Sonata in F Major, K. 332 I. Allegro, Mozart*

that does not stall at the end of every measure. The F in the fifth measure also begins the next phrase, creating an elided relationship, so the phrase extends even further than the first few measures outlined here.

The slurs in the Schubert sonata in figure 9.5 are similar to that of Mozart's in that they most often stop at the barline although the actual phrases do not. Analyzing melodic subphrases is always the key in understanding composers who use negative phrasing. If the Schubert example is whittled down to small subphrases and then built back up again, the life of the whole phrase becomes clear. The first step is outlining the sets of two notes that connect musically. These can be short-to-long rhythms (sixteenth note to half note, for example) or notes connected by tension or resolution. Although other possibilities exist for extracting two-note groups, the six in figure 9.6 seem to stand out.

The next step is to add longer note groups (fig. 9.7). In this passage, there is just one group of four notes in measures two and three. There are also two stand-alone notes at this level that do not immediately connect to any notes around them (fig. 9.8).

FIG. 9.5 *mm. 1–4a, Sonata in A Major, op. 120 (D. 664), I. Allegro moderato, Schubert*

FIG. 9.6 *mm. 1–4a, Sonata in A Major, op. 120 (D. 664), I. Allegro moderato, Schubert, two-note subphrases*

Combining the subphrase analysis and Schubert's original slurs results in one long continuous phrase (figs. 9.9 and 9.10). Analyzing the subphrases makes the small connections between notes and measures that spur energy and direction in this melody.

Using the same process as in the Schubert, it is easy to divide the opening bars of this Chopin nocturne into two- and three-note subphrases with a few stand-alone notes (fig. 9.11). Again, other possibilities exist, and performers will lean toward different interpretations, but one possibility is outlined in figure 9.12. In this example, listening for the pairings or other groupings of notes that create tension and resolution is at the crux of developing good subphrases. Once established, it is advisable to practice

FIG. 9.7 *mm. 1–4a, Sonata in A Major, op. 120 (D. 664), I. Allegro moderato, Schubert, three-note subphrase*

FIG. 9.8 *mm. 1–4a, Sonata in A Major, op. 120 (D. 664), I. Allegro moderato, Schubert, stand-alone notes*

FIG. 9.9 *mm. 1–4a, Sonata in A Major, op. 120 (D. 664), I. Allegro moderato, Schubert*

FIG. 9.10 *mm. 1–4a, Sonata in A Major, op. 120 (D. 664), I. Allegro moderato, Schubert*

FIG. 9.11 *mm. 1–4a, Nocturne in G Major, op. 37, no. 2, Chopin*

FIG. 9.12 *mm. 1–4a, Nocturne in G Major, op. 37, no. 2, Chopin, level one subphrases*

FIG. 9.13 *mm. 1–4a, Nocturne in G Major, op. 37, no. 2, Chopin, subphrases*

FIG. 9.14 *mm. 1–4a, Nocturne in G Major, op. 37, no. 2, Chopin, level two subphrases in three phrases*

the groupings separated from each other in order to hear all of the relationships at play (fig 9.13). The next step is to put things back together into three phrases (fig. 9.14). With the subtle inner connections in place, this phrase takes on a much more compelling interpretation as it spins out with purposeful direction.

MELISMATIC SUBPHRASES

What notes form subphrases in this long, melismatic section from the Haydn Sonata in E♭ Major (fig. 9.15)? Most long sixteenth and thirty-second note subphrases start on either the second or the fourth note. Once started, as with pieces written by Bach, subphrases tend to spin out in the same pattern indefinitely. In this case, each of the subphrases begins on the second thirty-second note (fig. 9.16).

Melismatic phrases such as this can sound chaotic and full of too many notes unless subphrases are developed. When every note expresses a relationship to every other note in context, listeners will hear the artistry and be grateful for the clarity it brings.

A more complex example is in Chopin's barcarolle in which finding sequential patterns helps determine the subphrases (fig. 9.17). It is important to organize long, melismatic passages like this one, which ultimately cover two-thirds of a page. Finding different divisions for subphrases is possible in this section, but these two examples point to one possibility. The subphrases here come in various lengths, some of which

(Allegro moderato)

FIG. 9.15 *mm. 40–42a, Sonata in E♭ Major, Hob. XVI: 52, I. Allegro moderato, Haydn*

FIG. 9.16 *mm. 40–42a, Sonata in E♭ Major, Hob. XVI: 52, I. Allegro moderato, Haydn, subphrases*

(Allegretto)

FIG. 9.17 *mm. 78–80a, Barcarolle in F# Major, op. 60, Chopin*

FIG. 9.18 *mm. 78–80a, Barcarolle in F# Major, op. 60, Chopin*

are unusually long with up to six notes each. Figure 9.18 demonstrates how these groupings materialize from the score into patterns. The interpretive focus can then shift from
individual notes to shaping the entire phrase based on these sequential subphrases.

Does this level of analysis harm the naturalness and spontaneity of a passage like this?
It depends. If a performer brings other qualities and skills to bear, such as great rubato,
suitable technique, and a sense of balance between the vertical elements, then, not at all. A
whole package of skills and emotion allows this sort of passage to move naturally. Analysis
simply provides a structure on which to hang one's expressiveness in performance.

ARTICULATION AND SUBPHRASES

Subphrases and articulation do not necessarily have to agree. In this Schumann piece, the
staccato markings do not preclude the piece from dividing into subphrases (fig. 9.19). The
drive of 6/8 still applies with its emphasis on beats one and four and upswings from beats
six and three. The note groupings should still have dynamic shape and energy regardless of
the articulation (fig. 9.20). The *sf*'s line up with the natural accents of the subphrases.

FIG. 9.19 *mm. 1–4a, Wilder Reiter from Kinderszenen, op. 68, Schumann*

FIG. 9.20 *mm. 1–4a, Wilder Reiter from Kinderszenen, op. 68, Schumann, subphrases bracketed*

FIG. 9.21 *mm. 9–10, Sonata in F Major, K. 332, II. Andante, Mozart*

Likewise, rests can be misleading as in this Mozart sonata (fig. 9.21). Here, the rests do not indicate the starts of new subphrases but are included in the existing one.

SUBPHRASES AND PATTERNS

At some level in this process of sorting out subphrases, patterns begin to emerge. They can be rhythmic or melodic in nature, or both as in this Chopin mazurka (fig. 9.22). The first level recognizes the initial small groupings (fig. 9.23), but the patterns almost jump off the page at the second level of analysis (fig. 9.24). At the third level, all four groups combine into one four-bar phrase (fig. 9.25).

FIG. 9.22 *mm. 1–4a, Mazurka in A♭ Major, op. 24, no. 3, Chopin*

FIG. 9.23 *mm. 1–4a, Mazurka in A♭ Major, op. 24, no. 3, Chopin, level one subphrase analysis*

pattern crosses Chopin's slur

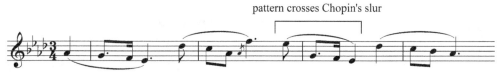

FIG. 9.24 *mm. 1–4a, Mazurka in A♭ Major, op. 24, no. 3, Chopin, level two subphrase analysis*

FIG. 9.25 *mm. 1–4a, Mazurka in A♭ Major, op. 24, no. 3, Chopin, level three subphrase analysis*

DYNAMIC CONTROL AND SUBPHRASES

Adding dynamics is the final step in developing subphrases. There are only a few guidelines, but they can be fussy and tricky to manipulate because of the small-scale range of the dynamics.

1. Generally, the first note of a subphrase is the softest.
2. Generally, energy of the subphrase moves toward a beat.
3. Generally, there is a crescendo to the beat unless the larger phrase structure is ending and coming to a point of resolution.

These short bursts of energy eventually add up to an entire phrase, but before that can happen, pianists must address another issue. Unlike almost every other instrumentalist, there is no dynamic control over a note once it is played. It decays. Within a phrase, any note following a long note must come in at the same dynamic level or even softer than the end of the long note. If this does not happen, the phrase is broken. Mastering this technique means that a pianist can create a phrase of any length, just a few notes or an entire piece (though an unlikely choice). In this Mozart sonata, mapping these dynamics with crescendos and decrescendos begins to resemble sausage links (fig. 9.26). It is important to remember that the dynamic differences between these notes are subtle, though. To make the four bars into one phrase, overall dynamics on a larger scale need to be cultivated. This should take the apex of the phrase into consideration as in figure 9.27.

Small-scale dynamics helps set everything into context in this Chopin impromptu (fig. 9.28). If not overdone, this level of attention gives motion and meaning to every note

FIG. 9.26 *mm. 1–5a, Sonata in F Major, K. 332, I. Allegro, Mozart*

FIG. 9.27 *mm. 1–5a, Sonata in F Major, K. 332, I. Allegro, Mozart*

(Allegro agitato)

FIG. 9.28 *mm. 5–6, Fantaisie-Impromptu, op. 66, Chopin*

of the line. It also makes the technical challenges easier to manage when every note is not at the same dynamic level.

Finally, the first few bars of the second movement of the Mozart Sonata in F Major provide an example with a variety of rhythms, perfect for a thorough analysis of subphrase dynamics. Figure 9.29 maps out one possibility for the right hand in these four measures.

FIG. 9.29 *mm. 1–4, Sonata in F Major, K. 332, II. Adagio, Mozart*

Subphrases are, perhaps, the most tedious part of score study. However, the effort to understand them and shape them with timing and dynamics makes for a performance in which every note has meaning. For this, it is worth diving in and discovering the value of expression on this small scale.

CHECKLIST FOR CHAPTER 9

- What slurs did the composer use?
  - Do they really define phrases?
  - Are they negative markings (a "do not break this set of notes apart" composer)? If so, what other notes should be included in the phrase?
- What are the subphrases? Is it possible to outline smaller subphrases of two to four notes by finding notes that create tension and resolution?
- Are there melismatic phrases? If so, where do the subphrases start and end?
- Are there subphrases that work regardless of articulations or rests?
- Are there patterns (melodic or rhythmic) that inform subphrases?
- What is the best way to organize small-scale dynamics around subphrases?

TEN

Transitions

Getting from Here to There

During transitions, harmonies are unstable, rhythm falls apart, and forward momentum can stall. Performing transitions effectively can be tricky and confusing. Even defining the term is problematic, but for the purposes of this chapter, it means the bridge from one substantial section of music to another.

THE LONG ROAD HOME

Composers use drama-producing techniques in transitions to heighten the clarity of longer forms. This is often achieved through long-term tension and instability followed by the emphatic arrival of V7 and, finally, I. It would be nice if things always adhered to this tidy description but it happens often enough that it marks a good place to start. Routinely, the feeling is that the composer has completely lost all sight of the original key of the piece and is "thinking out loud" in the compositional process and trying to get back on track. Despite their volatile start-and-stop and seemingly disorganized natures, the vast majority of long transitions are quite humorous when analyzed. If the performer recognizes this, playing them becomes a much easier task.

It makes sense that the most complex forms, which should persuasively delineate large sections, contain the most highly developed transitions. Of sonata form's three large sections, the exposition and recapitulation are highly regulated in terms of what key centers are explored and, to some degree, the character of the various themes. However, development sections tend to be harmonically chaotic as a matter of design, allowing composers to experiment wildly with keys and motives. Transitions at the ends of these sections

FIG. 10.1 *mm. 91b–103, Sonata in C Major, Hob. XVI: 50, I. Allegro, Haydn*

continue to be harmonically unstable as they begin to search for the correct V7-I cadence that could lead back to the recapitulation and restored tonic harmony.

Haydn, with his infinite sense of humor, experimented with a variety of key centers and registers before arriving at the recapitulation of this sonata (fig. 10.1). The variety of dynamics and registers separated by rests keeps this section lively. Haydn wrote something a little bit different with each small phrase, all of which fail to find the "right" chord—a G7, the V7 in CM. Because of these delaying factors, when Haydn finally starts to grab onto G (m. 99) followed by the G7 chord, the effect is extraordinary and this is, unmistakably, the bridge to the recapitulation.

Beethoven, in creating transitional materials, often reused motivic ideas found earlier in a work and then systematically disassembled them. Everything seems to fall apart bit by bit, until there is little left to do but stop, regroup, and consider what to do next. The first movement of the Sonata in F Major, op. 10, no. 2 contains a fascinating and complex transition. Here, not only does the thematic material disintegrate, but the harmonies twist about in such an odd way that the modulation from F minor to D major seems completely improvisatory, accidental, and unfortunate. This transition drags the key of D major into a false recapitulation before finally moving back to F major, the key of the piece. An analysis of this long section of music (fig. 10.2) shows how Beethoven took apart and reassembled this sonata from the end of the development section, through a false recapitulation (right theme, wrong key), to its true recapitulation (right key, wrong theme, in this case).

1. Left hand begins wandering off, changing harmonies as it steps downward.
2. A♮ appears, and with it, D minor is established. Sixteenth notes get stuck, triplets disappear, and a tentative character takes hold.
3. Beethoven tried an Asus chord, then an A7 chord, but abandoned both ideas by delaying further action with a rest.
4. False recapitulation! Main theme is in D major not in F major, as it should be. D major continues for twelve measures without any awkwardness that might signal the listener that it is in the wrong key. Finally, a second transition leads back to F major.
5. Another long but measured pause occurs just before this transition. The arrival of a G minor chord finally begins to address the problem of the wrong key. Once the B♭ appears, the two sharps from the rogue key of D major never reappear.
6. Cadence to C7, the V7 of F major. The following measures hammer home the impending key of F major, giving the key center time to stabilize.
7. Recapitulation begins in the correct key. The phrase mirrors the one starting in measure 123.

A V7 (F7) chord is found early in the next transition by Mozart, (fig. 10.3), but the recapitulation does not begin there. Mozart often introduced new thematic material in developmental sections, and this piece is no exception. Here, the transitional materials are from a trifling theme only recently heard and not found in the exposition. Additionally, he kept interjecting a G♭ into the bass, agitating the harmonies and effectively stalling the start of the recapitulation. There is a struggle between the right and left hands for harmonic control for several measures before the pieces moves into the main theme.

FIG. 10.2 *mm. 107–119a, Sonata in F Major, op. 10, no. 2, I. Allegro, Beethoven*

FIG. 10.3 *mm. 86–94a, Sonata in B♭ Major, K. 333, I. Allegro, Mozart*

1. Mozart introduced a G♭ to the bass.
2. Right hand—continuous sixteenth notes start, spinning around the same pattern several times.
3. Left hand—Resolution of G♭s to F begins to take hold.
4. Right hand—Chromatic melody destabilizes the phrase. Left hand stops playing.
5. Right hand—rhythm doubles and finally moves to the recapitulation, but not without one final jab at the harmonies with an E♮.

SHORT

Sometimes, transitions are short when thematic material seems to sputter out and stall as in this Schubert impromptu (fig. 10.4). Unlike sonata form, the straightforward nature of

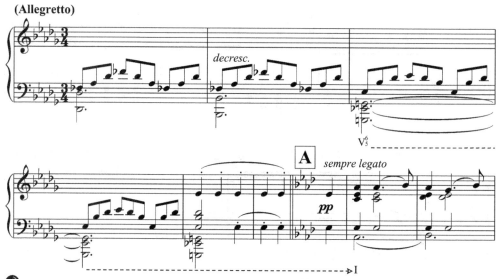

FIG. 10.4 *mm. 93–100, Impromptu in A♭ Major, op. 142, no. 2, Schubert*

ABA does not usually warrant a complex transition. In this piece there is no great drama or development of ideas, but the character must nevertheless quickly transform. This transition bridges the trio (B) to the return of the main theme (A), but the five E♭s seem hardly enough to move the music from the triplets of the trio to the more rhythmically sedate main theme. However, it is all Schubert wrote.

What makes this a viable transition is the slow slide into the V7 chord (E♭7) and its settling over a number of measures in the B section just before the main theme returns. Even though no ritardando is marked, a significant one is needed. Because the transitional material is weak, the pacing of the ritardando determines the effectiveness of this move back to the A section. A feeling of improvisation should dictate the rubato. Composers sometimes use elements of the upcoming main theme in their transitional materials as the repeated E♭s do here. It is as if the piece accidentally stumbles onto the main theme through the repetition of these notes.

MOTIVIC CONNECTIONS

Transitional materials also foreshadow a theme in Chopin's third ballade (fig.10.5). This simple, two-note motif shows up three times in the piece and serving as a unifying factor for the overall form. The motif's monophonic texture is a foil to the otherwise thick, chordal structures occurring in the rest of the piece and is easily recognizable in each recurrence. The falling two-note motif continues past the transition in every instance, forming the basis for the theme of the next section of music.

FIG. 10.5 *mm. 50–57a, Ballade in A♭ Major, op. 47, Chopin*

THE LAST THREE NOTES

Identifying subphrases can be helpful in deciding how to perform certain types of transitions. In Chopin's Revolutionary Etude, in ABA form, several transitions consist of sixteenth notes passages that run directly into the main theme with seemingly no preparation, as in this section that bridges the introduction and main theme (fig. 10.6).

For the first eight measures, Chopin failed to identify the key of the piece, C minor. At measure nine, he finally arrived at a C minor chord with an arpeggio in root position. Because this is such a pivotal moment in the piece, a carefully planned transition is crucial. Finding subphrases in long sixteenth note passages helps determine the shape of the larger phrase movement. Figure 10.7 shows one possibility. The last three notes of the introduction plus the first note of the A section provide a short but powerful bridge when played with a significant ritardando and a crescendo into the C of the next measure.

Focusing on the last three notes, usually bass driven, works well for short transitions because it makes it easy to slow the tempo enough to delineate form or to naturally bridge two diverse sections of music. Here, in Brahms's Intermezzo in A Major, this transition links two smaller, dissimilar sections in the form (fig. 10.8). A focus on the last three bass notes, combined with the first note of the next section, creates an effortless and effective transition (fig. 10.9).

In determining an interpretation for any transition, a pianist armed with a keen sense of improvisation and humor can effectively convey the surprises of uncomfortable key shifts and splintering motifs. Performance practice protocol must be followed but usually in transitional materials; the bolder the performance, the more interesting and captivating these sections become.

FIG. 10.6 *mm. 5–9, Etude in C Minor, op. 10, no. 12, Chopin*

FIG. 10.7 *mm. 7–10a, Etude in C Minor, op. 10, no. 12, Chopin*

(Andante teneramente)

FIG. 10.8 *mm. 21b–25, Intermezzo in A Major, op. 118, no. 2, Brahms*

FIG. 10.9 *mm. 21b–25, Intermezzo in A Major, op. 118, no. 2, Brahms*

CHECKLIST FOR CHAPTER 10

- What is the musical form of the piece?
- Is the transition at the end of the development section of sonata form?
  - If so, where does it begin?
  - Does the composer use humorous elements such as harmonic confusion, long rests, or fermatas?
  - Where does the composer firmly establish the V7 chord?
  - What stalling techniques does the composer use to delay the onset of the recapitulation?
- Is the form ABA or rondo?
  - If so, how long or short are the transitions between sections?
  - Where is the V7 chord?
  - How can rubato be used to make a smooth bridge between dissimilar sections?
  - If there are a number of transitions in a piece, does the motivic structure recur to provide a unifying theme throughout? How could one play them to make this clear?
- Is the "three-note rule" helpful in bridging sections more easily?

ELEVEN

"Staccato Means Short" and Other Myths

ARTICULATION

Students and some teachers hang onto the idea that staccato means "short" and/or believe that one type of legato fits every circumstance, without ever considering the rich possibilities that exist from one end of the spectrum to the other. Even though some have worked to create narrow definitions around articulation, there simply is no standard application of any of these markings.

The primary definition of staccato is "detached." Within the freedom granted by that single word is an array of possibilities that stretch from playing very short notes to holding them as long as is feasible without connecting to the next event. Conversely, legato means "smooth and connected," but just how connected should one play? Are there times when overlapping notes might be appropriate? The symbols found in figure 11.1 represent the range from staccato to legato in written music, but they only begin to hint at the prospects awaiting the curious musician. In performance, the range of staccato and legato effects is rich with endless nuances, as tempo and character come into play. After all, composers could only approximate in writing the articulation they had in mind.

STACCATOS

In scores, staccatos may be represented any number of ways including dots, wedges, lines, words (i.e., sempre staccato), or by nothing at all. In reality, the definitions of these symbols and markings are all the same with a preference by composers to use one or another. In some schools of thought, the wedge staccato is promoted as having a crisper attack than the dot. Although this approach may work sometimes, it is not appropriate for every

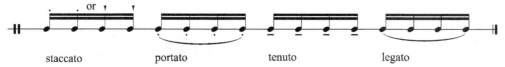

FIG. 11.1 *Range of Symbols used from staccato to legato*

phrase that contains them. With any articulation, a performer has some leeway in deciding what sounds best.

Three Beethoven examples demonstrate a variety of staccatos. In the first, the fast tempo and staccatos on sixteenth notes lead to their quick and short execution (fig. 11.2). Clearly, there is no other way to play them.

In the second, Beethoven combines both dots and rests to indicate staccato playing. It takes more time to write eighth notes and eighth rests than quarter notes with staccatos, so why did he choose this option? Perhaps he wanted to rule out the possibility of holding each chord longer than an eighth note, so chose the fussier writing style. However, if the chords are too short they are not substantial enough for the listener to hear them. Generally, chords need more time on the ground than single notes, requiring a different approach to staccato. In this example, playing with a slightly elongated, sticky feel allows the chords to have enough "meat on their bones" so that the audience understands the harmonic progression at play.

In figure 11.4, the tempo and character of the piece and the legato notes that share this phrase point to a long execution of the staccato notes. Short notes would sound out of place in this somber adagio. Other challenges present themselves in this passage as well. There are notes not marked staccato that should be detached. For instance, the Es

FIG. 11.2 *mm. 1–4, Sonata in E♭ Major, op. 31, no. 3, II. Scherzo, Beethoven*

FIG. 11.3 *mm. 1–4, Sonata in G Major, op. 14, no. 2, II. Andante, Beethoven*

FIG. 11.4 *mm. 1–4, Sonata in C Major, op. 2, no. 3, II. Adagio, Beethoven*

in the bass of the first measure should be released with the A in the right hand. If they do not, the passage can sound messy. As there is a staccato in the right hand, a performer will probably play the left hand detached by default and precision in the release of these notes together tidies up the texture. Another issue is that composers often did not indicate whether the last note of a slur should be staccato or not. In two-note slurs, the second note is usually staccato, even though it is not marked. Here, the second notes of the first two measures in the right hand should match the articulation of the notes that follow.

PORTATO

Portato, a term borrowed from bowing, is a way of indicating a longer note that is still detached or staccato. Portato is written with either staccato marks under a slur or staccatos in combination with tenuto marks. This section of Brahms's Rhapsody in G Minor follows the bombastic opening page of the work (fig. 11.5). Its mysterious quality is lost if the portato Ds are played either too short or too legato. Brahms used this in-between articulation in an attempt to communicate the right texture and mood; an amorphous, spongelike approach to playing should serve this passage well.

There are other instances in which a portato is not written by the composer, but all of the elements in a passage suggest it as an appropriate interpretation. In Schumann's Wichtige Begebenheit, the wedged chords can be played with a portato touch – long, but

(Molto passionato, ma non troppo allegro)

FIG. 11.5 *mm. 20b–22, Rhapsody in G Minor, op. 79, no. 2, Brahms*

FIG. 11.6 *mm. 1–4a, Wichtige Begebenheit, from Kinderscenen, op. 15, R. Schumann*

separated (fig. 11.6). If the chords are played too short, they will not represent the character of the piece, which translated means "important event." Conversely, the music and mood command a crisper sound than legato playing would allow.

TENUTO

Surprisingly, the symbols for both portato and tenuto appear more infrequently in the literature than one might expect. The tenuto marking, when used, generally indicates to a performer to hold a note or chord for its full value, and in rare instances, it is used as an accent mark. It is up to the performer to determine the composer's intentions. As an indication of a hold, it is especially effective when a rest follows because of its positive affect on rhythmic pulse. In a sense, tenuto is a negative marking, suggesting that the note should not be too short. To confuse matters further, composers use this mark for other reasons, too, as can be found in the Pavane pour une infante défunte by Ravel. In the closing section, he uses tenutos liberally, not as accents or to indicate full value of notes but simply to highlight the melody in a tangle of voices in the score (fig.11.7).

LEGATO

The indications for legato playing are varied and inconsistent. Although slur marks can indicate legato playing, they may also have other meanings attached to them. Occasionally, the words *sempre legato* may appear in a score. Even dolce or cantabile can imply legato

(Assez doux, mais d'une sonorité large)

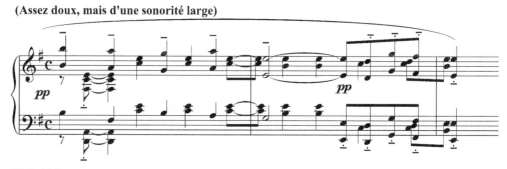

FIG. 11.7 *mm. 68–70a, Pavane pour une infante défunte, Ravel*

FIG. 11.8 *mm. 1–3a, Sonata in F Major, K. 332, III. Allegro assai, Mozart*

playing. Sometimes there is no indication at all. Besides these inconsistencies, the range of legato playing is expansive. A performer needs to experiment to find the most effective style and sound for each circumstance.

For instance, in this Mozart sonata, an overly exuberant legato would dampen the crispness of the opening phrase (fig. 11.8). Notes that barely touch one another will communicate the fiery and brilliant nature of this piece.

Conversely, the opening to this Beethoven sonata movement would sound improper unless the legato is well oiled with notes that not only touch but also occasionally overlap. Beethoven provides some clues to this, particularly the carefully notated finger-pedaled bass melody and his use of the word *grazioso* in the tempo marking (fig. 11.9). Even though this is a minuet movement, it is also the slowest movement of the sonata and should project some of the gravitas normally reserved for andantes and adagios. Although both examples are legato passages, their differences demonstrate the extremes ranges of the spectrum of playing "smooth and connected."

RESTS

Developing interpretive strategies around the spaces in music is intricately tied to articulation. Rests can be ignored or given exact or inexact values depending on their context. The point at which a note stops and the rest begins creates a pulse and can heighten clarity in a fast, rhythmically driven section of music if played precisely in time. When strictly observed, the rests in this Mozart sonata create a sharp, clean sound (fig. 11.10).

FIG. 11.9 *mm. 1–4a, Sonata in A♭ Major, op. 31, no. 3, III. Menuetto, Beethoven*

(Allegro)

FIG. 11.10 *mm. 23–30, Sonata in B♭ Major, K. 333, I. Allegro, Mozart*

(Adagio)

FIG. 11.11 *mm. 8b–10, Sonata in F Major, K. 332, II. Adagio, Mozart*

Deemphasizing rhythm through an imprecise treatment of note lengths works if the intent is to lessen the impact of the rest, particularly in works with slow tempos such as this Mozart sonata (fig. 11.11). If the rests arrive on time, the rhythmic rigidity makes it difficult, if not impossible, to maintain the melodic character of the passage. Most of the time, faster tempos require strict values for notes and rests, and slower tempos call for a looser, more relaxed interpretation.

Staccatos always create rests, although this is probably not something a performer normally considers. It is possible to plan the release of notes in a way that creates a strong rhythmic impulse as in figure 11.12. The quarter note staccatos, played as eighths with eighth rests, give this rhythmic gesture additional muscular strength.

DYNAMIC ACCENTS

Composers used a wide variety of marks to communicate dynamic accents. Though there may be some slight differences in execution, the point is to draw attention to a note or a group of notes. An accent should not be overplayed, however, and must relate to the ongoing dynamic of a section of music (fig. 11.13).

The first, a tenuto, is used only occasionally as an accent mark as mentioned earlier. *fp* can indicate an accent, or it can mean a sudden change of dynamics. *sf* and *sfz* are

FIG. 11.12 *mm. 21–22, Sonata in B♭ Major, K. 570, I. Allegro, Mozart*

FIG. 11.13 *Commonly Used Accents*

interchangeable and are often most effective when a dynamic accent is combined with a slight delay of attack (agogic accent) as discussed in chapter 8. *rfz* may mean to accent a single note or chord, but most frequently it indicates that a section of music needs to be reinforced, or played more forcefully.

DYNAMICS

Dynamics have much more to do with character than with decibels. Consider this example from Beethoven (fig. 11.14). Beethoven has set up a type of slingshot effect with the

FIG. 11.14 *mm. 17–22a, Sonata in F Minor, op. 2, no. 1, III. Prestissimo, Beethoven*

growling, repeated chords that eventually break off into the descending scale. The scale should be loud, perhaps with a martellato attack, but it is hardly possible or desirable to play the single-note scale as loudly as the chords that precede it. Here, Beethoven's dynamics are geared toward creating an aggressive attitude and not for suggesting that everything in this example should be played at the same dynamic level. There is a point past which the piano is unable to offer up a good quality sound, so care should be taken not to overplay the instrument.

Dynamics are more guidelines than hard information. With this subject more than most, it is important to understand how composers intended for their written dynamics to be understood. For instance, composers such as Mozart and Haydn generally wrote only p and f, with scant sprinklings of other dynamic markings. For them, moving from p to f does not necessarily mean the dramatic change it would in Beethoven. There is a shift in the dynamic level, but more importantly, it signals a change of color, texture, or treatment. When preparing dynamics for these composers, it might be helpful to think in terms of a change in orchestration or color, rather than of opposing dynamics. The new section should be softer or louder, but certainly not as much as it would be for works from a later period. From Beethoven onward, composers notated dynamics in a more direct and detailed manner.

Control over dynamics rests largely in one's skill at voicing. The ability to put every note in its place through weeding out the "unnecessary" ones, developing good bass melodies, and focusing subphrases bring an enormous range of expression to even the softest dynamics.

Experimenting with the wide ranges permissible with dynamics and articulations will greatly expand the interpretive resources available to every performer. Ultimately, this exacting, and often exhausting, work will bring a depth of expression and clarity to one's playing that is not otherwise achievable.

CHECKLIST FOR CHAPTER 11

- Staccato, portato, tenuto
  - How short/long should a note or chord be in a given passage?
  - Are there chords in play?
  - If so, the playing length of them should be long enough so that the harmonic progressions can be heard.
  - What is the tempo? Generally, the faster the music, the shorter the staccato can be. Slower tempos require a "sticky staccato," even when they are not marked portato or tenuto.
  - What does the composer mean when writing a particular tenuto mark? Is it that the note or chord is accented, held to its full length, or is it a way to direct attention to a melody or bass melody?
- Legato
  - What does the composer use to indicate legato playing? Slurs? Terms?
  - What type of legato is needed for a given passage keeping in mind that the range goes from nonlegato to overlapping notes.

- Rests
  - Is this a fast, rhythmically driven piece? If so, should the rests be strictly observed?
  - Is this a slow, lyrical piece? If so, rests should be inexact when possible to subvert accents caused by the release of notes.
  - Are there times when a note with a staccato mark could have an exact rhythmic cutoff?
- Dynamics
  - Is an agogic accent combined with a louder dynamic useful for *sf* or *sfz* markings?
- Are these types of accents reflective of the surrounding dynamics, or are they too loud?
  - What character, orchestration, or mood does a dynamic in a certain passage bring to mind?
- How can the dynamic be communicated effectively?

TWELVE

Pedaling

A pianist should disregard almost all pedaling indications in scores. Even if they appear in a composer's autograph copy, it is almost never clear who wrote them. In addition, pianos have changed over the centuries, and some markings may not effectively translate to a modern instrument. Even if one has carefully worked out the pedaling for a given piece, each piano and concert hall is different and one has to adjust in a flash to changing circumstances. A detailed discussion of the history of pedaling along with performance practice suggestions can be found in Joseph Banowitz's *The Pianist's Guide to Pedaling* (Indiana University Press, 1992), listed in the Further Reading section at the end.

THE DAMPER PEDAL

The damper pedal is much more than an on-off switch and is capable of creating a whole realm of expression in music not possible without it. Matters of pedaling rely more on the ear than the foot, and the nuances are endless.

Some quick facts about using the damper pedal:

1. In general, the earlier a piece was written, the shorter the pedals.
2. Using the pedal can create inadvertent accents. Quick and careless on-and-off motions will cause mechanical noises, whooshing sound on the strings, and/or tapping noises if the foot is not resting on the pedal. Also, every time the pedal is changed, the sound of any held notes will jump to a softer dynamic.
3. The dampers on a piano stop at some point in the treble clef. The note where this stops is not the same on all pianos and may affect the way one pedals.
4. It is easier to use long pedals if the melody is rising rather than falling.
5. It is easier to use long pedals if the melody is in an upper register rather than in middle register of piano.

Every pianist needs an arsenal of skills at his or her command. Three basic types of pedaling—syncopated, catch, and accent pedals—are the ones used most often.

SYNCOPATED PEDALING

Syncopated pedaling is the most common of the three and the one taught earliest in lessons. The following two exercises help to train the ear along with learning the physical aspects of this type of pedaling (figs. 12.1 and 12.2). In each, it is impossible to play legato without using the pedal. Although some method books allow for haphazard pedaling at the beginning (leaving syncopated pedaling until later), students must learn early on that the pedal goes down after they play a note or chord and not simultaneously, even though the pedal marking looks as though it should. This awareness helps to encourage good physical and aural habits from the beginning.

If the student is not able to play chords, this exercise is a good alternative (fig. 12.2).

CATCH PEDALS

In the following example, Beethoven wrote a slur over the chords in the bass clef (fig. 12.3). Making these legato without the use of the pedal is impossible. If one does not plan pedaling in a purposeful way, though, problems with a messy melody begin to appear.

FIG. 12.1 *Synchronized Pedaling Exercise*

FIG. 12.2 *Synchronized Pedaling Exercise*

FIG. 12.3 *mm. 4b–8a, Sonata in F Major, op. 10, no. 2, I. Allegro, Beethoven*

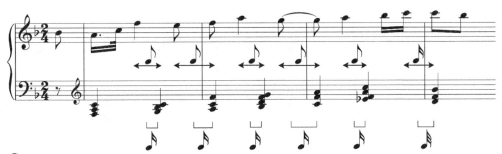

FIG. 12.4 *mm. 4b–8a, Sonata in F Major, op. 10, no. 2, I. Allegro, Beethoven, pedaling added*

FIG. 12.5 *mm. 1–2 Sonata in F Major, K. 332, II. Adagio, Mozart*

FIG. 12.6 *m. 2, Sonata in F Major, K. 332, II. Adagio, Mozart, pedaling added*

Catch pedaling is closely associated with syncopated pedaling but is much quicker and is for assisting legato playing in tricky spots. Generally, the length of time the pedal is depressed should be roughly half of the shortest note values at play (fig. 12.4). When done properly, the legatos of both the right and left hands are preserved without the overlapping of any notes.

Catch pedals are practical in cases in which repeated notes make it impossible to play a phrase legato. In this Mozart sonata example (fig. 12.5), the gap between the repeated As has to be reconciled in the second measure to make the legato of the two measures match.

A quick catch pedal fixes the problem created by repeated notes (fig. 12.6).

ACCENT PEDALS

To assist the volume and timber of loud chords, accent or strengthening pedals are invaluable. The damper pedal is depressed and released exactly with the beginning and ending

FIG. 12.7 *mm. 149b–152, Sonata in F Minor, op. 2, no. 1, I. Allegro, Beethoven, pedaling added*

FIG. 12.8 *mm. 18b–24, Sonata in B♭ Major, K. 570, I. Allegro, Mozart*

of the chords, so the foot and hands work entirely in tandem. This gives the chord or chords a fuller and louder sound as in the ending of the sonata movement by Beethoven found in figure 12.7.

This technique is also useful for less powerful chords when a broader sound is desired. In this transitional section into the second theme, a rhythmic approach to playing and pedaling works well (fig. 12.8). The chords and pedals whittled to eighth notes, with eighth note rests in between, sharpens the rhythmic effect of these measures.

LONG PEDALS

"Change the pedal when the harmony shifts" is basic advice given to beginning and intermediate pianists. Hymn playing comes to mind and is a good way to practice listening for harmonic shifts and for realizing that it is not a good idea to pedal through right-hand stepwise motion. However, in other music one rarely finds a hymn's simplistic texture. Longer and longer pedals, sometimes over changing harmonies and stepping melodies, are possible when voicing is addressed and bass melodies pulled out of textures. As always, it is vital to understand performance practice in order to make palatable choices, so pedaling that would be appropriate for late romantic music will not work in early classical repertoire. The range of possibilities expands throughout tonal music with some works from the romantic era allowing for very long pedals at times. The famous Rachmaninoff G Minor Prelude provides a good example (fig. 12.9).

FIG. 12.9 *mm. 35–38, Prelude in G Minor, op. 23, no. 5, Rachmaninoff*

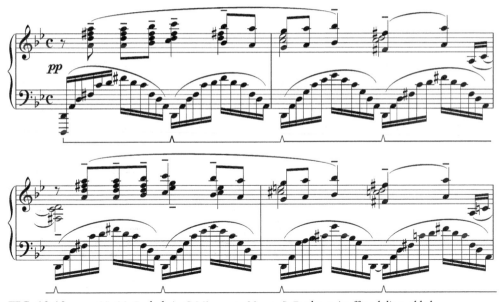

FIG. 12.10 *mm. 35–38, Prelude in G Minor, op. 23, no. 5, Rachmaninoff, pedaling added*

It is clear, on looking at the score, that the low Ds found in the bass on beats one and three are the fence posts for this section. However, in each measure the melody moves in a stepwise pattern. Although one instinct might be to change the pedal with the right hand as it moves upward, this is late romantic music, so this might not be necessary. Rachmaninoff wrote a dynamic of ***pp***, and without saying so directly, gave the pianist a lot of latitude with the pedal. If the tops of the right-hand chords are brought forward with the other notes played as softly as possible (and they need to be in this soft dynamic) and the left hand voiced to a whisper, except for the Ds, pedaling at the half measure should work without distraction (fig.12.10).

(Molto passionato, ma non troppo Allegro)

FIG. 12.11 *mm. 13b–17, Rhapsody in G Minor, op. 79, no. 2, Brahms, bass melody marked*

Using this type of long pedal means that a pianist has to voice a piece carefully by planning ahead of time what will come to the forefront and what will stay mostly unheard, or the result will sound messy and unclear, even with the most romantic of music. Driving forces in music must always be recognizable; in this case, it is Rachmaninoff's exquisite melody.

FIG. 12.12 *mm. 13b–17, Rhapsody in G Minor, op. 79, no. 2, Brahms, pedaling added*

FIG. 12.13 *mm. 1–4, Claire de lune from Suite bergamasque, Debussy, pedaling added*

FIG. 12.14 *mm. 26–29, Toccata from Pour le piano, Debussy*

At first glance, the similar-looking passage from Brahms might lead one to the same conclusion of changing the pedal with the bass melody (fig. 12.11).

One time through, however, and it is obvious that this will not work because of the change of harmonies within the longer pedaled sections. The logical and more frequent pedaling for this section creates a gap in the texture when the bass D from beat one no longer speaks, leaving the phrase lightweight on the third beat of each bar. There is little to be done to even this out (fig. 12.12). Sadly, it is not always possible to find an ideal pedaling and voicing combination, and a pianist has to make the best choices with the tools at hand (and foot).

Sometimes it is possible to close similar gaps that occur with necessary pedal changes. In Claire de lune, Debussy took care of possible melodic voids at the beginning of each measure by writing tied notes over the barlines (fig. 12.13).

It is necessary to pay close attention to the ties in this type of situation when a pedal change would cut these notes short. Even without ties, sometimes using a finger pedal can keep unforeseen gaps from occurring such as in this fast passage from another Debussy piece (fig. 12.14).

Holding the first few notes of the right hand longer than written gives the performer some leeway as to when the pedal can engage. In figure 12.15, the pedal can be played anywhere in the first half beat without the melody developing odd gaps. Without holding the fingers down, the pedal must strike before the end of the first sixteenth note to have the same effect, difficult even if one knows a piano well.

FIG. 12.15 *mm. 26–27, Toccata from Pour le piano, Debussy, finger pedaling*

MORE SUBTLE USES OF THE DAMPER PEDAL

The pedal does not always need to be pushed all the way to the floor. With the pedal fully pressed, the dampers are completely up, inviting the resonance of every string. As the pedal releases, the dampers begin a descent back to their resting places and their role as dampening devices. However, in between a pedal fully up and fully down is a world of possibilities. With the pedal slightly depressed, the dampers brush the surface of the strings, deadening the resonance a little. In this Chopin nocturne, a very long pedal can be used in the transition section if it is hovering just at the point at which the dampers are barely making contact (fig. 12.16). Although often called a "half pedal," any fraction in pedaling is possible,

FIG. 12.16 *mm. 59–66, Nocturne in B♭ Minor, op. 9, no. 1, Chopin, pedaling added*

FIG. 12.17 *mm. 15–20a, Sonata in F Minor, op. 2 no. 1, I. Allegro, Beethoven*

resulting in a large array of color possibilities. No compositional markings exist to indicate this, so it is up to the performer to seek out the appropriate pedaling and sound.

This Beethoven sonata demonstrates another place where a partial pedal is useful (fig. 12.17). The first two presentations of this theme are easy to play legato, but the third, in octaves, needs help. There is no pressing need to use the pedal in full force, and doing so would take more time than using a shorter-dipped pedal in this fast tempo. This little bit of help is all the passage needs to maintain a legato sound.

The flutter pedal is also a good tool to have. In this passage from Beethoven's op. 109 Sonata, the sound would be too dry without any pedal, but a pedal on each septuplet disrupts the flow with its constant interrupting and singling out each beat as it goes by (fig. 12.18). Pressing the damper pedal, perhaps to its halfway point,

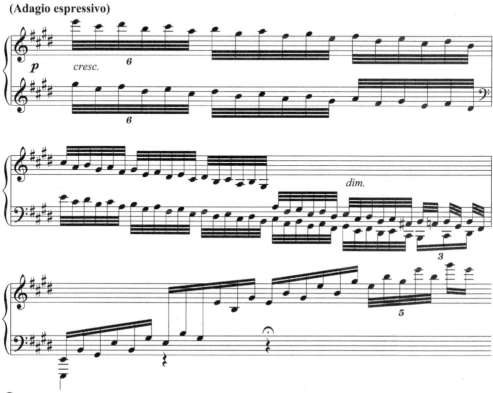

FIG. 12.18 *mm. 63b–65a, Sonata in E Major, op. 109, I. Vivace ma non troppo, Beethoven*

then bringing it back up without completely releasing it at various times (and not on the beat) will keep the passage well oiled without creating an unpalatable muddle of sound.

THE UNA CORDA PEDAL

The una corda pedal is used when a change of timbre is desired. It is carelessly known as the "soft pedal," but under no circumstances should it ever be used to cover up the lack of skilled soft playing. On a grand piano, the action slides the hammers out of their normal alignment with the strings. The ungrooved portion of the hammer strikes at fewer strings than before, which creates a muted sound that happens to be softer. Using this pedal is reserved for two special occasions. The first is when a composer indicates it by using u.c., una corda, II Ped., or the occasional con sordina. Composers do not always use a marker for the release of the pedal, but when they do, a t.c. (tre corde, meaning "three strings") appears. Even when there is no written una corda, a pianist can decide to use it to set a section of music apart as special. The pedal has such a startling effect on the timbre, it is as if a different instrument is being played. A common use is to set major and minor presentations of a theme apart as in this Mozart example (fig. 12.19).

THE SOSTENUTO PEDAL

The sostenuto pedal, a late nineteenth-century invention, is rarely indicated in music. It is hardly used at all and is not even factored into the building of most upright pianos. Mechanically, it holds the dampers off the strings for any notes played before the pedal

(una corda)

FIG. 12.19 *mm. 21–22 and m. 25, Sonata in F Major, K. 332, II. Adagio, Mozart*

(Assez animé et très rythmé)

FIG. 12.20 *mm. 6–9, Prélude from Pour le piano, Debussy*

is depressed, unlike the damper pedal, which lifts every damper on the piano. It works best for long pedal points in the bass when there is a clear shot at grabbing the note (or sometimes a chord) in a clear way without snagging other, harmony-interfering notes. The prelude from Pour le piano provides a good example of a passage that benefits from its use (fig. 12.20).

The sostenuto pedal is put down just after the As are played and before the damper pedal is used. It does not need to be replayed and can stay down as long as the pianist wishes the A pedal point to be heard. In this case, there is no need to lift the sostenuto pedal until nineteen measures into this passage.

The use or nonuse of pedals almost entirely depends on individual expressivity and how one wishes to communicate a particular piece or passage of music. The examples here are simply ideas to guide one in understanding what is possible and may lend some imagination to the process of developing an extensive pedaling arsenal. Starting with a concept of sound and then finding out how the piano can deliver it properly puts the horse before the cart.

CHECKLIST FOR CHAPTER 12

- Damper Pedal
  - When was the piece written, and how might this affect pedaling choices?
  - Are there extraneous mechanical noises when one pedals? If so, what are they, and what are the causes?
  - Where do the dampers stop on the piano being used, and how might this affect pedaling choices?
  - Does the syncopated pedal sound smooth with no gaps or overlaps of notes?
  - Are there places where catch pedals can help create a legato effect where the fingers cannot?
  - Are there places where strengthening or accent pedals can enhance the sound of chords?
  - Are there places where a long pedal could be used to connect bass melodies?
  - If so, is it possible to keep direction and voicing clear enough to use it?
  - Are there places where holding a note longer than its value and over a pedal change can help to cover an otherwise noticeable gap in the texture?
  - Are there places that could use a half pedal or flutter pedal?
  - How does the piano and/or performance hall change pedal usage?
- Una corda pedal
  - Is the una corda being used for a change of timbre and texture rather than to create a softer sound?
- Sostenuto pedal
  - Is the pedal clean or are there extraneous nonchord tones that should not be there?

Afterword

The intricacies of music are endless, and the creative process of each musician will pull musical ideas together differently. Building a repertoire of interpretive skills that flow naturally in one's playing and teaching is the obvious next step, so some suggestions for moving forward may be helpful. Perhaps working through the chapters chronologically with a new piece would be a place to start putting the skills learned here into practice. Another suggestion would be to identify a troubling area in an old piece and to apply some of the ideas from the appropriate chapter. Maybe, as a teacher, using the checklists will help kick-start a student's enthusiasm for learning a new work.

While the information and examples here offer the tools to play expressively with good instincts that can be further developed, this book may not necessarily lead to historically accurate playing. Emphasis here is on a broader understanding of the mechanics of interpretation. How a piece was performed during the era of its composition on the available instruments of the time may not be how a twenty-first-century pianist on a modern piano for contemporary audiences chooses to play. Learning more about performance practice will inform the pianist how ornaments worked for each piece and what the limits were for rubato and dynamics, for example, at the time of composition. Ultimately, it is our fortune as musicians to decide how we will bring music to our world.

Some may say that music interpretation at the piano is serious, hard, and daunting, but this book has laid the groundwork for a basic grasp of interpretational skills. By following the principles and techniques suggested here, a musical work can be engaged on a deeper and more meaningful level, and at the same time, curiosity can lead the performer beyond these suggestions to more advanced interpretative techniques.

There is boundless freedom in having the ability to choose, often in the moment of a live performance, any number of substantial options that can communicate with and draw in an audience. With the ability to choose your own interpretation, you own the power and uniqueness of your performance, which will connect with those who hear you play.

Glossary with Annotations

TEMPO—SLOWING DOWN

Ritardando, Rallentando, Cédez, Slargando

- Slow down, becoming slower.

Note: Some composers attach negligible differences to the terms, but all four basically mean the same thing.

Smorzando, Morendo, Slentando, Perdendo, Calando

- Gradually slow down and get softer.

Note: The definitions have different nuances, but at the piano, the application is the same.

Sostenuto

- Sustained but occassionally with the implication of slowing the tempo.

Ritenuto, Meno Mosso

- Slower.

Note: Sometimes the term ritenuto is used in place of a ritardando.

TEMPO—SPEEDING UP

Accelerando, Poco a poco a tempo, Stringendo

- Gradually speed up.

Note: Stringendo has the added characteristic of agitation or tension.

Più mosso, Animato, Stretto, Agitato

- Suddenly faster.

Note: Stretto and agitato have the added characteristic of agitation or tension.

DYNAMICS AND ACCENTS

fz, *sfz*, *sfp* Forzando, Sforzando

- A sudden accent within the prevailing dynamic. *sfp* is immediately followed with a dynamic of piano.

Note: The best way to interpret accents and dynamics is to play with a slight accent while delaying the attack. The agogic, or delayed, accent creates the illusion of a stronger dynamic.

rf, *rfz*, Rinforzando

- Reinforced.

Note: In practice, there is usually a short section of music that needs to be emphasized as opposed to a single note or chord.

Agogic

- An accent based on time rather than dynamics. In this book it is used to indicate the delayed attach of a note or chord.

COMPOSITIONAL DEVICES

Alberti Bass

- An accompanimental figure that changes a three-note chord into an eighth- or sixteenth-note pattern, generally lowest note, highest note, middle note, highest note.

Deceptive cadence

- A cadence point, often a V^7—vi movement, that suddenly shifts the harmonies to a "resolution" chord the listener would not ordinarily expect.

Note: Usually, if the unexpected chord is set apart by a slight agogic accent, it signals to the audience the special quality of the moment.

Elided phrases

- When the resolving note or chord at the end of one phrase also begins the new phrase.

Note: In nearly every case, the first phrase needs to resolve both rhythmically and dynamically, often into a new measure, before moving to the second phrase. The second phrase should grow out of this "low point."

Fermata

- A symbol used to indicate that a note or rest should be held longer than indicated.

Note: Although some attach a specific duration to a fermata, for example, to hold it for 1½ times longer than indicated, it is more of an individual decision based on good taste. A slight break between a held note or chord and the next event creates clarity for the listener. Because the fermata is indeterminant in its duration, the break is like a breath before the following phrase.

Fortspinnung

- A spinning out of thematic and rhythmic material used mainly in the Baroque period of music.

Hammerstroke

- A chord played loudly at the beginning of a piece that announces the key, usually without thematic significance.

Melisma

- A term borrowed from vocal music referring to a single syllable that lasts through many notes. In instrumental music, the term is applied to melodic phrases that continue for some length of time in an unchanging rhythm (often in straight sixteenth notes) that can be subdivided into subphrases.

Pedal point

- A held note or the repetition of the same note in the bass, regardless of the harmonies above it. This effect is often, but not always, intended to imitate a drone instrument such as a bagpipe or hurdy gurdy.

Picardy third

- The major third in a major chord used at the end of a minor-key piece.

Polyrhythm

- The simultaneous use of two different sets of rhythms that do not derive from the same subdivision, such as duplets in the right hand with triplets in the left hand.

Structural ending

- A strong V-I cadence (usually with root position chords) toward the end of a work, often at the coda.

Note: This calls for special voicing to bring the dominant voice forward while pushing the other into the background.

TEXTURES

Monophonic Music

- A single line of music without accompaniment.

Homophonic Music

- A predominant melody supported by the other voices, as in hymn writing. Sometimes known as melody and accompaniment. Generally, the voices move at the same or near same rhythm.

Polyphonic Music

- All voices are treated equally, and all contain melodic material. They overlap to create a complex web of melodies as in fugal writing.

Incidental Counterpoint

- Occurs in music that is mainly homophonic but features interesting material in a voice that is not the melody.

ARTICULATION AND ATTITUDES

Ad Libitum, A Piacere, Tempo Rubato, Cadenza

- All indicate a freedom in tempo and expression.

Appasionato, Sfogato

- Grand, passionate expression with emotional intensity.

Note: Can indicate an increase in rubato and volume.

Cantabile, Dolce, Espressivo, Teneramente, Tranquillo, Grazioso

Note: These are found with slower tempos and softer dynamics. There are nuances to their meanings, but the effect for each at the piano is similar. Cantabile and dolce have the added meaning of bringing out the melody, but this is good advice for the other expressive terms here as well.

Légèrement, leggiero

- To play lightly.

Note: A light, nonlegato touch is often appropriate with these indications.

Martellato, Strepitoso

- *Martellato* means "hammering," and *strepitoso* means "noisily."

Note: These notations are best when played with a nonlegato, heavy touch. They are mentioned together here because they present occasions when overplaying the piano might be appropriate. This distinguishes them from marcato ("marked") and pesante ("heavy"), which are one level below in dynamic and never indicate the production of an ugly sound.

Sotto Voce, Mezza Voce

- Sotto Voce—"under voice," Mezza Voce—"half voice"

Note: Although most dictionaries will differentiate between these two terms, in piano music, they are nearly interchangeable. Each requires constraint in its performance technique. This effect is achieved if the melody is not voiced and all vertical notes are played at the same subdued dynamic level.

Common Stylized Dances or Dance-Related Forms

Core Baroque Suite Dances	
Allemande	(German origin) Duple meter time, in moderate tempo, binary form. Usually has an upbeat or upbeats and almost always consists of a composite rhythm of sixteenth notes. Later, it meant a piece "in the German style" but did not have any dance form relationship.
Courante	(French, "running") Triple meter, varied rhythms, moderate tempo, imitative texture, binary form. Sometimes employs a hemiola rhythm.
Corrente	(Italian, "running") Triple meter, binary form, fast. Generally, the corrente has a faster tempo than the courante and features a steady, composite rhythm, such as eighth notes. Bach labels many of these courante, so one has to look for clues in the music to determine which type it is.
Sarabande	(Spanish origin but the characteristics significantly changed over time) Triple meter, binary form. Slow, often with an emphasis on beat two, binary form.
Gigue	(English origin) compound meter—usually 6/8, fast tempo, imitative, binary form.
Other Stylized Dance Forms	
Minuet	(unclear origin) Triple meter, slow to moderate tempo and usually paired with a trio. Later, when a faster tempo was needed, a scherzo was substituted for the minuet. All three are in binary form with repeats, but upon the return of the minuet (or scherzo), the repeats are not taken. Minuet, menuet, minuetto, and menuett are all the same.

Mazurka	(Polish origin) Triple meter, often with the natural accent shifted to the second beat. There are three types of mazurkas, each with different tempo and characteristics.
Polonaise	(Polish origin) Triple meter, moderate tempo. Can have a characteristic rhythm of an eighth note, two sixteenths, followed by an eighth note
Waltz	(unclear origin) Triple meter, moderate tempo. Occasionally in later romantic music, an anticipation of beat two is appropriate. Generally, the emphasis is on beat one with a secondary nod to beat three.

Further Reading

PERFORMANCE PRACTICE

Neumann, Frederick. *Ornamentation in Baroque and Post-Baroque Music with Special Emphasis on J. S. Bach*. Princeton, NJ: Princeton University Press, 1983.

Brown, Clive. *Classical and Romantic Performing Practice 1750–1900*. Oxford, UK: Oxford University Press, 1999.

Rosenblum, Sandra. *Performance Practices in Classic Piano Music: Their Principles and Applications*. Bloomington: Indiana University Press, 1988.

INDIVIDUAL COMPOSERS

Badura-Skoda, Paul. *Interpreting Bach at the Keyboard*. New York: Oxford University Press, 1995.

Badura-Skoda, Paul. *Interpreting Mozart: The Performance of His Piano Works*, 2nd ed. New York: Routledge, 2010.

Geiringer, Karl. *Brahms: His Life and Work*, 3rd ed. Cambridge, UK: Da Capo Press, 1984.

Kinderman, William. *Mozart's Piano Music*. New York: Oxford, 2006.

Rosen, Charles. *Beethoven's Piano Sonatas: A Short Companion*. New Haven, CT: Yale University Press, 2001.

Rosen, Charles. *The Classical Style: Haydn, Mozart, Beethoven*, exp. ed. New York: W. W. Norton & Company, 1998.

Samson, Jim. *Chopin*. New York: Oxford University Press, 2001.

Tovey, Sir Donald. *A Companion to Beethoven's Pianoforte Sonatas*, rev. ed. London: ABRSM (Publishing) Ltd, 1999.

Wolff, Konrad. *Masters of the Keyboard: Individual Style Elements in the Piano Music of Bach, Haydn, Mozart, Beethoven, Schubert, Chopin, and Brahms*, enlarged ed. Bloomington: Indiana University Press, 1990.

Walker, Alan, ed. *The Chopin Companion: Profiles of the Man and the Musician*. New York: W. W. Norton & Company, 1973.

PEDALING

Banowetz, Joseph. *The Pianist's Guide to Pedaling*. Bloomington: Indiana University Press, 1985.

GENERAL KEYBOARD LITERATURE

Hinson, Maurice. *Guide to the Pianist's Repertoire*, 3rd ed. Bloomington: Indiana University Press, 2001.
Kirby, F. E. *A Short History of Keyboard Music*. New York: Free Press, 1966.

GENERAL MUSIC INTERPRETATION

McGill, David. *Sound in Motion: A Performer's Guide to Greater Musical Expression*. Bloomington: Indiana
University Press, 2009.

Index